Praise for *Hot Water*

'In *Hot Water* Nadine Dirks tells us exactly what it's like to be battling your body and South Africa's public healthcare system. Memoir and manifesto, this is a bold and essential mediation on the politics of chronic pain, misogynoir and womaxhood.'
– Dr Kate Law, Africanist and feminist historian who specialises in modern South African and Zimbabwean history

'I am thrilled to endorse Nadine Dirks's remarkable book, *Hot Water*. This heartfelt and courageous memoir takes readers on an unforgettable voyage through the challenges, triumphs and resilience of someone living with endometriosis.
'Nadine has masterfully woven together her personal experiences with this debilitating condition, offering readers an intimate glimpse into the physical and emotional toll it takes. Her candid storytelling not only educates but also empowers those who may be facing a similar journey.
'What truly sets this book apart is its unwavering commitment to raising awareness about endometriosis. Through Nadine's storytelling, we gain a deeper understanding of the struggles women face when battling this often misunderstood and underdiagnosed condition. It serves as a vital resource for patients, loved ones and healthcare professionals alike.
'*Hot Water* is a testament to Nadine's resilience, determination and advocacy. Her ability to transform pain into power is an inspiration to us all. If you're looking for a story of hope, courage and the strength of the human spirit, I wholeheartedly recommend this book. It's a powerful reminder that, even in the face of adversity, we have the power to overcome and make a difference.'
– Candice Chirwa, mental health activist, thought leader and author of *Perils of Patriarchy* and *Flow: The Book about Menstruation*

'*Hot Water* takes us on a compelling pilgrimage. Nadine shines the spotlight on the stark realities of social injustice, systematic violence in healthcare and the need for daily self-renewal through resilience.'
– Landa Mabenge, founder and managing director of Landa Mabenge Consulting (Pty) Ltd and author of *Becoming Him: A Trans Memoir of Triumph*

First published by Jacana Media (Pty) Ltd in 2023

10 Orange Street
Sunnyside
Auckland Park 2092
South Africa
+2711 628 3200
www.jacana.co.za

© Nadine Dirks, 2023

All rights reserved.

ISBN 978-1-4314-3350-6

Also available as an ebook.

Cover design by Chantelle Warburton
Set in Ehrhardt 12/15.5pt
Printed by Inside Data
Job no. 004075

See a complete list of Jacana titles at www.jacana.co.za

Hot Water

Nadine Dirks

For my ancestors; whose voices still echo in the kraal

Contents

Acknowledgements	9
Health, care and crisis	11
My body, my traitor	21
Prejudice, cut me open	35
All my life, I had to fight	57
How to birth your IUD and an endometrioma	67
Just a bietjie white supremacy and a dash of privilege	83
Regrets and losses	93
The waiting game	101
The scent of death lingered in the air	109
There were complications	127
This tief is trying to take me out	151
Not this shit again!	159
Recovery 3.0	175
Getting my house in order	199
A last goodbye	215

Acknowledgements

Camagu! To my ancestors.

First and foremost I would not have been able to write my story without the support, guidance and help from my family and friends. I would like to thank my parents for dealing with me glued to a screen, and ensuring I've eaten or bringing me cups of tea to soldier on. To my Hatta, thank you for always praying for me, telling me you're proud of me. I am indebted to you for raising me to have the feminist values I have today: not to mention for drilling down the need for education. Thank you to my sister Nicole for allowing me space in your home to write, and for pushing me and thinking of ways to market my book, I am so grateful for you allowing me to vent and lose my mind every now and then. Nicole, thank you for always holding me accountable. To my brother Matthew, who always showed up to every medical appointment or procedure. Matthew would use his scrubs, reputation and charm in hospitals he worked in to find me and hold my hand.

I could not have done this without my best friend Jamil, who is my God-given solace. Jamil has nurtured me, loved me, fought for me, and helped me create this book. Thank you for doing the work, when I couldn't carry the baton. Thank you to Nadia Goetham, my

Mama hen, for the opportunity to write and work with you.

A special thank you to my high school English teacher Lesley Mally, without whom I would not have believed I could create art out of my words. Thank you to my therapist Candice, for helping me through the traumas I've faced but also always being in my corner, cheering me on. Your help and investment in me is insurmountable. To Ayesha Toyer and Thabisa Nondzube, thank you for being examples of what I could be if I wanted to. Your academic prowess, friendship and wit has enriched my work and life.

Thank you to incredible role models and friends throughout my life like Lebogang Mashile, Professor Barbara Boswell, Makhosazana Khanyile and Tebogo Rametse who have held me. To Mase Ramaru for always providing sisterhood, for sharing knowledge, and just knowing how to have a good time. To Alaric, thank you for being available and ready to help me with headshots or troubleshooting my laptop to make sure I could create. Your acts of service are so appreciated, your presence in my life makes every day a good day.

Thank you to my second mom, my aunt Michelle Barnabas and her family for constantly celebrating me. Without Michelle's assistance in raising my sister and me, we would be poorer for it. You've added so much intelligence, creativity and talent to our lives.

To women like Dr Anna Mokgokong who walks bravely without a path already created for her, you make me a better woman. Thank you to my friend Dineo Maboe-Khambule who is more like family than a friend; there aren't words for the support you've given me. Without a simple call from you to help me change my mind, I may not have been here today. To my Rakgadi Matlhogonolo Maboe and Mmane Morongwi who prayed for a miracle over my life and succeeded, "amen amen amen." Thank you so much to Professor Lindsay Clowes for always having room for me, it is invaluable. Thank you for the bottom of my heart.

I would like to extend a thank you to everyone who has ever published my work, anyone who has ever impacted my life. A huge thank you to the Jacana team and everyone who has endorsed and worked on this book.

Health, care and crisis

FOR GIRLS WHO ARE, LIKE ME, from Hanover Park – a small township in Cape Town infested with gang violence and poverty – the world can seem incredibly small. It is like being within a society, within a bubble, that very little of the outside world seems to penetrate and reach. We are all born in the community day hospital, raised in the community and go to school because it is a legal requirement. Before it was a legal requirement, many did not finish even primary school, especially girl children.

Generally speaking, even then, the chances of escaping and experiencing life outside of the bubble seemed impossible, and almost laughable to even consider. You are bound to duty, poverty and Black tax. Tertiary education is seen as an aspiration for white people, not us – never us. When I was younger, it was not even a conversation – so much so that I did not even know that it was a possibility. After we finish school and try to find a job, the next step, as with the rest of the sacraments for girl children from the Flats, would be to get married, and have children – ideally in the order specified. If you switch the order up, you will raise eyebrows and be judged severely by everyone – from the priest to the neighbourhood drunkard and even the community moms.

Your worth as a girl child is seen in key things – respectability,

European beauty standards, your ability to perform wifely duties and, lastly, the functionality of your womb. Even as a child, your mind is filled with ideas of motherhood, and how it is a blessing to have children. Your job is to be fruitful and multiply while relying on God to make a way. This concept always made me laugh internally although I never verbalised it – having children and relying on God to provide for them. It sounded strange to me, considering how so many people and their children were living in poverty – I didn't understand it, and thought maybe there was a special number of children you had to have before the whole making a way thing starts to kick in. There is no margin for error, no wiggle room, no negotiation... And woe to those who are not fruitful and who do not multiply, because surely ... surely ... they are cursed by the Almighty with lifelong spinsterdom?

Sexual and reproductive health is taboo. We don't talk about it at all, so it does not exist, right? You are better off assuming babies come from the mountain because asking questions about them is shameful. We don't talk about our genitals or sex organs, we use euphemisms, even as adults, and there are no conversations about why some people's ovens don't work as they should, apart from the occasional community skinner about how so and-so's husband ran off, apparently justifiably, because so-and-so's oven was not working. Women's worth is in their ovens and their ability to make dough rise without mishaps. And yes, by oven ... I do mean uterus. To add insult to injury, there is no situation wherein it is justifiable for women to walk out on their marriages, even if the reason is something their husbands could control – unlike infertility. As a woman, you are then instructed to carry your cross. I guess it is as the saying goes on the Cape Flats: 'Meat is meat and a man must eat.'

In the middle of winter in July 2014, when I was 19 years old, I was rushed to the hospital on my GP's orders – he was not entirely sure what was wrong with me but knew it was dire enough to give me a letter to be seen at the emergency room at the local hospital.

I was feeling feverish, nauseous, exhausted and had extreme pain – especially on the right side of my body. The nurses and hospital staff took pity on me because I looked like I was near death because of the pain. I was immediately admitted and spent the night and early morning undergoing a series of tests and scans to get to the bottom of what was causing my strange symptoms. I was then informed I was not allowed to eat – not that food was even on the agenda in that noisy, smelly and overcrowded ward. Soon thereafter, I was told that I needed to have an emergency surgery as they had located a mass on my right ovary from a scan. I was terrified and had no idea what to expect or what it could be – I had never had any kind of surgery before.

I woke up, groggy from the anaesthesia, and was back in the enormous post-surgery ward. It seemed that everything in there was in various shades of white – white linen, white uniforms, white walls. The light was unnervingly bright to me and, suddenly, my doctor appeared out of nowhere, leaning over the railings of my hospital bed. She made no attempt to prepare me, sugar-coat or even check that I was fully conscious before she started to speak. She stopped speaking, or I stopped listening, I may have slightly blacked out again and then I heard her say 'you have endometriosis, really, really bad. It is unlikely that you will ever have children.' I don't remember responding, or acknowledging what she had said, and felt myself slipping back into an anaesthesia-induced stupor as her face faded away in my mind's eye.

Even through the numbing effects of the anaesthesia, I felt a heaviness – the feeling of despair and hopelessness had already started to creep in. My entire world shattered around me, as I lay in my hospital bed attempting to physically recover while being torn apart emotionally and psychologically. It felt brutal, disheartening and inhumane. The doctor's bedside manner, in retrospect, is one of the coldest, most violent experiences of my life. She let me know my life, as I knew it or imagined it, would never be the same again with about as much empathy and emotional range as someone ordering a coffee. I don't suppose the need for counselling or proper emotional support is important for girls like me.

The air was sucked out of the room and everything felt thicker, darker, strained. I had no idea how I was going to survive, how my family would be able to help me gain access to the lifelong healthcare I would need, or how I was going to keep myself sane, trying to cope with being a teenager who was chronically ill. The torment of wondering how you can possibly make yourself smaller, less of a burden, how you can deal with everything on your own as a teenager is the kind of anxiety no one should have to deal with.

I woke up several hours later. Back from surgery in an unfamiliar ward, it was the middle of the night, my abdomen felt like I had been sliced open – which I later learned was what happened – and the woman in the bed next to me seemed inconsolable. I could not move to console her, and so I tried to speak to her, while attempting to alert the nurses without startling everyone else in the ward who seemed to be fast asleep. She told me that she had just miscarried and was afraid that her husband was going to leave her because it had happened before. She told me that his family were very traditional Zulu people and said that they had advised him to leave her because of her fertility issues. She was devastated. I was 19 and could not seem to find the words to fix her world – as I lay there, unable to move, groggy from morphine, and dealing with my own conundrum of my oven. How do you even begin to fix a faulty oven?

This is what the healthcare system does for us – the absolute bare minimum – not even so much as a plan to get people some necessary support and coping mechanisms. It also quickly puts things into perspective, maybe not immediately, but certainly as an afterthought, that our lives and bodies are not valued in the same way as others are. If you are lucky enough to find yourself born in the middle of an intersectional jackpot that crosses all aspects of gender, race, class and the rest, you may find your experience to be very different. Your healthcare is likely to be multi-disciplinary, involving all aspects of what you need – be it emotional support, a gynaecologist, an endometriosis specialist – and depending on where the endometriosis is located – a bowel surgeon. The privileges allotted to you become things that you are accustomed to – as easy as calling your doctor when you are feeling under the weather, scheduling appointments via email, or even getting weekly vitamin B injections for the never-ending fatigue that comes with endometriosis.

So, there I was, in my Mitchell's Plain hospital bed, counting my sacraments to see how many I had managed to fulfil at 18. I had never been particularly keen on respectability and many, including family, friends, the community and even teachers, had commented on it throughout my childhood. My parents had raised resilient, feminist, warrior daughters – the very opposite of the 'waiting for a knight in shining armour' type of woman. There was nothing 'ladylike' about me – nor did I even slightly attempt to be ladylike. I swore, cursed the patriarchy and frequently found myself fighting. Tjerrr... I sighed mentally at the thought of having to perform respectability and ladylike-isms to be accepted, taken care of or desired by someone's son. Okay, but at least I had the school aspect going for me, I had finished high school just the previous year. My oven was faulty and I was not going to live in a world of euphemisms filled with buns in ovens or the lack thereof. Another issue arose, even with education – a young woman must toe the line very, very carefully. Too little education and she is unsuitable as a partner, but too educated? Oh no, now you have gone too far! You risk being undesirable by possibly emasculating the men around you who absolutely need to be more educated than you.

I remember praying, rosary in hand – thanks to my grandmother who ensured I had my rosary with me at all times. My poor grandmother's very Catholic expectations hung onto me, threatening to crush my windpipe like a massive boulder. My grandmother was a firm believer in our duty as Catholics to be fruitful and multiply – evidently my grandmother was not the only Catholic who believed this. She and most of Latin America would agree. I had no idea how I was going to keep from disappointing her, especially as her favourite granddaughter (my sister may argue this point deeply), when she found out that I was in fact not going to be able to do what she had expected of us. How was I going to tell my 90-something-year-old granny that the doctors had said there would be no buns in the oven? I lay there, in my hospital bed, for what felt like an eternity, with those lights that never seemed to go off, be it day or night, and the smell of hospital – that strong mixture of antiseptic, medicine and the ever-so-faint smell of urine. I started to speak slowly and intentionally. I asked Mother Mary for help, for comfort, for support, for the feelings of despair to leave me. After all, my granny always said to think of Our Lady as our Heavenly Mother who we could call for assistance at any time. And so I prayed to be taken away in the hospital bed so that I would not burden my family who had already sacrificed, worked hard and suffered their entire lives. I prayed for their hurt to stop and for me not to be the cause of their hurt. I took it on me, in my spirit, to save my loved ones from me and my defectiveness and yet, I woke up the next morning to the sound of nurses changing shifts and somehow turning those bright fluorescent lights even brighter as a reminder that this was it... I was stuck, we were all stuck, no one had heard my prayers and lifted the weight. I guessed that maybe even Our Lady was pre-occupied at a private hospital – maybe as a patient at a private hospital, you get the number to send Our Lady of the Rosary a WhatsApp message directly.

    I had not yet applied to a tertiary institution. I was eating my youth with a gap year, or so I thought, but really, in retrospect, my gap year was just surgery, diagnosis and recovery. I like to think it was my ancestors' clever plot to keep me going with school, knowing that I would have possibly had to drop out if I needed the surgery later on. I needed to then consider: would I go back to school and explore what was waiting for me, or was it going to be entirely impossible physically, mentally and emotionally? Should I instead find a means to secure a marriage, what with being *defective* and all? The thought of being defective could not even seem to find a comfortable spot in my mind or body to fester and grow. I would not let it.

The assumptions of defect became apparent to me very early in my journey, from the look of sorrow, pity and grief in the eyes of others. Although often well meaning, their sorrow and pity was not for me to carry, it was a projection of their own thoughts, feelings and what society has fed us about ourselves as girl children who become women. It is the biggest fear so many have – and, oftentimes, the fear people have is not because of their desire to be parents but more the quandary of 'what will people say?' or the ingrained concept that marriage and children are the only ways to live a 'normal' and 'fulfilling life'. Somehow, this seems to only apply to women. I have never heard the question posed to the boys or men around me but always to the girls and women. Every Christmas, Easter and family gathering without fail.

You know how Oprah has what she calls 'aha moments'? Well ... because I am me and not Oprah, in typical me fashion I do not have those. What I do have is 'mxm moments'. I am seemingly always a little bit queer. I realised that no matter what I did, what I said, how I lived my life – it would not matter. What people think or perceive is exactly that – a perception, one drawn from their lens of the world around them, and no matter how hard any of us try to fit the narrative, to someone else, you will always be off and there will always be something to discuss. My square would never fit into someone else's circle and vice versa – so does it even matter? I mean, why should it? 'Go forth and do you' became my mantra for my life.

So, in short: was I going to let my worth as a person be defined by my uterus? No. Was I going to let my worth, life and potential be defined by being a suitable wife to someone – yet again based on my body's ability to conceive? Hard no. Do I intend to use someone else's ruler to measure myself? Certainly not. Therein started the journey for me: truly soul searching and asking myself what it is that I wanted without the hindrance from society, my community, and even my family. Suddenly the pressure to attempt respectability and graciousness as a pre-requisite faded away – it was more about me and what nourished me. I was going to choose me and do what felt right in my soul.

That moment was defining for me, and it did not come easily. It felt like it happened overnight, but it did not. I had to work for it, unlearn, rethink, create and imagine. There were no templates for how to be powerful, unyielding, gracious and fearless for girls and women like me. The templates that existed were burnt down in the trash fires that we know to be colonialism, slavery, apartheid, the dop system and more – the girls and women who have been taught that our worth lives in our bodies; the girls and women who have been told that taking care of ourselves and that self-love is a radical concept – something that comes from selfishness. I had to truly go deep within myself, into my soul and provide myself with the softness I had been taught to give freely to others even when I was running on empty. I have spent many times beating myself up for not availing myself, not yielding, not giving in to a world and society that was set up to eliminate us as soon as we were of no use or, God forbid, realised our worth.

I had to fight myself for myself. The absolutely bizarre concept I held that I was to avail myself to everyone but not to myself had to be shattered to survive endometriosis. I had to learn to say no and stick to it. Saying no feels as unnatural as taking the day off to tend to my own wellbeing. I had to reflect on my path – past, present and future. I had to nurture myself, take away the 'should' and 'have to' demands I made of myself, the unkindness I showed myself. The way I had cursed my body endlessly – screaming incessantly at myself about how I was a 19-year-old and my body should work like a 19-year-old's. Furious and frustrated about how I could not go out drinking and clubbing with my peers, annoyed that I could not hike Table Mountain, saddened that I sometimes needed naps when everyone else my age could go on and on all weekend. I was heartbroken by the feelings of not being able to do what 'normal' people my age did, so much so that I even forgot to check in with myself. Surely, had I taken the time to check in with myself before full on meltdowns about being unable to do certain things, I would have sooner come to the realisation that I didn't even enjoy those things and would not have liked it, endometriosis or no endometriosis. I don't like to be sweaty – so you will not find me hiking a mountain unprovoked or in a club where it is generally hotter than hell for sport.

That is how it is, though – the whole reason we should not covet other people – you start yearning and throwing your toys out of your cot in a childish fit over things you, in your truest form of yourself, would not like anyway. Seeing other children with it, however, suddenly makes us think to ourselves that… 'yhu, even me, I want'. Do you really? It is a strange concept having to ask myself those pertinent questions, but if I was going to continue breathing, fighting, learning and evolving for my greatest good and hopefully learn something along the way – it was vital. I realised I could not have a fulfilling life wanting for things, running after things or living a life without introspection. Introspection for me was the difference between getting what I wanted for my highest good and just getting what I want.

My silver lining appeared there – not in pretending that this was some kind of divine lesson and miracle bestowed unto me because I could handle it. None of that whole 'you are not given more than you can take' stuff. I am not deluded either, it sucks big time, and some days are harder than others. Some days feel like the ocean has decided to swallow me whole and thrash me around in a riptide, some days are not too bad, some days I still want to scream hysterically and ask 'why me? Ugh! What did I do to deserve to be in such debilitating pain?' Other days, I look at myself in the mirror and smile, and say 'uyanyisa, wena sisi … look at you, making the pots'. My life, just like everyone else's, has its ebbs and flows – and I have learned to tackle it, scream at it, laugh my head off in sheer joy, swear in five different languages and question God. More importantly, I have learned that I am pretty extraordinary. I have my back, I call myself out on my nonsense and I have accepted the days where my body demands I sit things out, drink water and nap – and I don't even feel guilty for needing to take care of my body and soul.

My body, my traitor

I GOT MY PERIOD AT 11 YEARS OLD. My parents had already informed me what a menstrual cycle was and what I could expect. The usual conversation about the uterine lining shedding each month, how uncomfortable it can be and the unwanted effects, but nothing could have prepared me for my first period. The night before I got my period, I had lost my appetite, I felt irritable, I had a throbbing headache, nausea and severe pain. I recall being curled up on my sister's bed, crying about not wanting to go to school the following day because the pain was so severe. My mother, tea in hand, agreed a day off school was necessary.

The following morning, it happened – I woke up in debilitating pain. I had trouble walking, dizziness and heavy bleeding. The onset of my endometriosis symptoms was almost immediate. I dreaded the thought of being hijacked and held hostage by my own body, inhibiting me from being the care-free child I once was. All the things I enjoyed doing like playing with my friends and being active suddenly came to a screeching halt. My period lasted for two weeks at a time; I bled profusely and would go through a pack of pads in a day. My bleeding caused severe anxiety because it was hard to control and happened so fast, within an hour my pad would be soaked rapidly in a vivid red flow through my school uniform.

I cannot begin to describe the countless times this has happened to me, and the aghast look on people's faces conjuring an array of inappropriate reasons for my symptoms. I eventually resorted to using two pads at once, kind of like a diaper, in the hopes that I could avoid some of the staining.

My symptoms continued to worsen to the point of the school secretary keeping my father's number on speed dial. Without fail, each month I would pass out on the school stairs because of dizziness and loss of blood. I would experience such severe nausea that I would be unable to get to the bathroom in time resulting in a projectile vomit of lunch. The pain was so severe that it blurred my vision. I experienced constant issues with my bowels such as chronic diarrhoea or constipation. Walking or doing too much physical activity resulted in the worst symptoms. My lower back persistently felt as if there was a dull pain that lulls but never disappears. My teachers were largely unsupportive and always assumed the worst as if for some reason I was playing sick to go home or avoid physical activity.

I distinctly recall sitting in my classroom during a lesson and feeling as though I were soaking wet on the lower half of my body. The air in the room made me gag and the sun blazing in through the shutters made me feel even more feverish. I asked my teacher if I could be excused to go to the bathroom, and she looked at me and snidely remarked, 'Missy, you had a break an hour ago, if you wanted to go to the bathroom so badly, you should have gone when you had the time.'

I sulked back into my chair, anxiously hoping the lesson would end shortly so I could go to the bathroom, despite the fact that I had indeed gone to the bathroom already during my break. Soon the pain hit me like a tonne of bricks and I felt weak. I had to rest my head on my desk and stare at the trees blowing in the wind to keep myself calm. My best friend looked over to me and noticed I looked unwell, and she blurted out to the class: 'Can't you see Nadine is unwell? Why won't you allow her to go to the bathroom?'

My teacher, red in the face, infuriated with my friend for advocating for me, conceded and said I could be excused. I slowly pushed my desk away from my chest and proceeded to steady my feet and stand up to go to the bathroom when I felt eyes on me. Everyone gasped, my teacher's mouth dropped, my best friend became hysterical attempting to help me. My baby blue and white pinafore school dress was crimson from the waist down. I looked down in horror and tied my blazer around my waist to hide my bloody embarrassment. My heart raced so severely that sweat dripped down my face. I thought I was dying.

During the Easter holidays in my first year of high school everything shifted. I remember a sudden onset of strange symptoms I had never experienced before in my life. I felt like I was coming down with the flu, I had an awful backache, I was irritable, lost my appetite and threw up every single thing I ate. The next morning, I woke up feeling like my head would explode given the opportunity and the dizziness was so severe that it made it difficult to see straight or walk to the bathroom a few metres from my bedroom. My parents were so worried that my dad resorted to carrying me around to get me out of bed. We drove around for hours trying to find a doctor open for consultations during Easter.

My mom had cushioned the backseat of our family's white Uno and laid me down while we looked for medical assistance. At some point my parents decided to stop at a Clicks to see if the pharmacist or nurse on duty could help me. The pharmacist told my mom that the nurse wasn't in and gave us details of a nearby GP instead because he suspected I might have meningitis. My dad carried me back to the car and we got to the GP who thankfully was open and seeing patients. He examined me thoroughly, bending my limbs, examined my eyes and checked the skin on my belly for dehydration. He seemed concerned and advised that I needed an antibiotic injection, as well as a course of oral antibiotics, pain medication as well as medication to control my nausea and vomiting, and said that I needed to stay indoors and under supervision because he could not solely diagnose meningitis based on a physical examination but couldn't rule it out either. He softly tugged at the skin on my belly and announced that I was dehydrated, likely because of the vomiting and nausea. He proceeded to make notes and pull out a roll of bright red stickers to attach to my antibiotics to remind me not to stop the medication even if by some miracle I started to feel better. He then rolled me over facing the wall, which had a poster of the spinal column that I studied to distract myself from the cold alcohol wipe. First the pinching and then burning sensation on my left buttock started as the doctor injected the antibiotics. He swiftly pressed down firmly to stop any bleeding while he grabbed a plaster to put on the small hole.

'There you go, Ms Dirks… Now you have to come back to me in two days, and you have to try your best to hydrate, even if you drink little sips of apple juice.' Most importantly, he reiterated, 'Whatever you do, don't go outside and socialise, and don't stop taking your antibiotics at any point.'

I just nodded, desperately wanting to leave because my eyelids felt heavy and my body felt worn out from the journey around the Cape Flats to find assistance. I just wanted to go back to sleep. When we were leaving, I saw the doctor pass my mom a small white envelope and he instructed her to keep it with her and to take me to the closest community healthcare centre and produce the letter he had written should my condition suddenly worsen or if any complications arose after hours.

The doctor's offices had a set of stairs and my parents helped me down, so we could go home as instructed and hope for the best. I was tucked into bed, with my supply of medication and the curtains were drawn because I had been struggling with a severe headache. I fell asleep but was suddenly awoken by the sharpest back pain ever. The pain was so brutal that I woke my parents up screaming bloody murder. I couldn't talk and explain the pain other than that it felt like I was being stabbed. My parents hurried to get me to our local community healthcare centre. I lay on the back seat, looking up at the bit of starry sky I could see and felt like I was falling asleep. We arrived at the clinic and were told that we could not park inside because it was after hours, even though it was cold and my parents had a sick child in the car. I had to be carried in by my dad, while my mom argued with an admin clerk who was obviously not eager to assist over the Easter weekend. She explained to my mom that we would have to sit in the cold, drafty waiting area. The wooden seating banks were so old they had splinters, the floors looked as if someone had mopped it with dirty water, and any medical assistants were behind bars and we had to wait to be seen. The clerk told us that they were only dealing with emergencies and that took priority over my case. We waited until we were eventually called to a large, open-plan room with a few beds, desks and chairs; there were a few patients who were bloodied and unconscious.

One particular bed stood out to me that had a pool of blood on it but no patient. The nurse, a stocky middle-aged coloured woman who seemed like she had seen it all, called me in to sit down with my mom who handed her the letter and explained the past few days to her. She made notes in a manilla folder and looked up over her bifocal glasses occasionally. The nurse then asked me to go to the bathroom and bring her a urine sample before continuing with other physical examinations. I took the old baby food container from her which I had to use to collect my urine. The doors on the bathroom didn't have locks that worked, it smelled like urine, and the floors were dirty and sticky beneath my feet. I had to be careful not to sit down because the plastic toilet seat had cracks in it. I tried to squat but my legs were weak so I did what I could, and as my luck would have it there was no toilet paper or soap present to wipe and wash myself. The taps at the basin didn't work except for one and it only produced cold water.

I handed the sample to the nurse, who put a plastic strip in it and then looked at me and asked my mother to leave the room. I didn't want my mom to leave, I felt alienated and scared, and I felt sick but the nurse insist she needed to be alone with me. My mom left and assured me she was right outside and would be back shortly, the nurse asked me, 'Nadine, why is there blood in the urine you gave me?'

I looked at the container holding my urine and couldn't see any blood present, I was confused and asked her, 'What blood? There's no blood in there?'

The nurse questioned me about whether someone had been bothering me or hurting me or doing something I didn't want them to do. In retrospect, I respect the nurse's decision to separate me from my mother because if I had been raped, which she was trying to figure out, I probably wouldn't have wanted to say it in front of my mom for fear of crushing her. Once the nurse was satisfied and concluded that the blood present in my urine wasn't because of trauma but because I was menstruating, she called my mother back into the room. She explained to my mother that the blood in my urine was because of my menstruation, but that she couldn't explain my symptoms and so she felt it best that she refer us to Groote Schuur Hospital.

We arrived at Groote Schuur's emergency unit in the dead of the night with two letters, one from the GP and one from the nurse, and waited for hours before being seen. I watched an old man a few seats from me clutch his chest and there was a sudden commotion from the staff before they wheeled him away. Then the doctor called my name and we made our way through. The doctor examined me thoroughly and took blood samples, and explained that in order to check for meningitis we needed to do a lumbar puncture. My mom asked me how I felt about it and I expressed fear but she told me we needed to find out what was wrong. I was taken to a small ward which, while meant for eight beds, had double the amount. The spaces in between patients were so narrow that only one person could stand at the bedside to attend to patients. The ward had all kinds of people. The smell in the air was awful and reminded me of the smell of a dead animal. I was given an intravenous drip to help with my dehydration and pain, and for the purpose of antibiotics.

The doctor asked my mom to help get me into a sitting position. My feet dangled off the bed towards my mom, who held my arms, as the doctor behind me prepared for the lumbar puncture. I was terrified seeing the needle, which looked like a knitting needle more than a surgical needle. The procedure hurt and made my legs kick forward as a reflex. I tried to breathe until the doctor finished and I was allowed to lie back down. I felt some relief from the pain medication and drifted to sleep as we waited for the results of the lumbar puncture. I woke up to the sunlight beaming in through the windows, and soon after the doctor arrived with my mom. He said, 'Unfortunately, Mrs Dirks, your daughter's lumbar puncture results are inconclusive because it contained blood in the sample. We would need to redo it but if it is meningitis – she has the right medication…' My mom was infuriated and said to the doctor that there was absolutely no way she was going to consent to another lumbar puncture. She told me, 'Let's go home and rest. This place will make you sick!'

My parents tried their best to support me and seek out medical care given the circumstances around the life experience of Black people in South Africa. My parents were beaten by apartheid police at school, resulting in a lack of quality education, minimum resources, land displacement and poverty. They didn't have a chance to better their lives and secure high paying jobs to cover costs like medical bills, leaving me at the mercy of the public healthcare system wherein people fall through the cracks. You are at the mercy of the staff and so there are limitations in asserting yourself and your needs as well as getting appropriate treatment; and being treated with dignity is a luxury. The standard of medical diagnosis is subpar especially for less common illnesses. My parents took me to any GP, local government clinic, Clicks clinic – anywhere they could find. My mom advocated for me to be prescribed a contraceptive to keep my period away as an attempt to control some of my symptoms but her pleas were never heard. I remember the sorrow in my mom's voice as she begged the doctor who was behind his desk, in a white coat with his hands folded, smugly looking at my mom as if she was being foolish. He then interjected with a chuckle, 'My dear, she is too young for contraceptives. It is normal to have pain when you menstruate. Besides, giving her a contraceptive sends a message that it is acceptable to be promiscuous.' Now research indicates a contraceptive would have assisted me but because of my then GP's misogyny he ignored not only my wishes, or my mom's wishes, but more importantly my symptoms. Minimising my entire experience as one that is normal.

I continued to see GPs who tested my urine for infections, physically examined me, monitored my blood pressure, just to be sent home with 15 generic paracetamols which did nothing for the pain. Eventually my parents, at their wits end, asked the doctor for a referral letter because we had hit a wall and it was clear we had run out of options. The doctor agreed and gave me a letter to go to my closest community healthcare centre. My parents opted for the clinic in Hanover Park because that is where I was born and it was close enough to where we lived and where I went to school. The area where the clinic is located is dangerous, an epicentre for gang violence, robberies and gun-related crimes. The clinic looked ancient, the walls were a godawful shade of mint green that had faded and stained over the years, the wooden benches were falling apart and filthy, the system worked on a 'who you know' basis and by that I mean those who know admin staff get preferential treatment. The queues were long and would take hours, the entire clinic smelled faintly of antiseptic, urine and a mixture of various foods people had brought along for the long stay. The clinic was always full, and always loud with people shouting about what they were selling – chips, cooldrinks, sweets – or people arguing with each other about who got in line first. The clinic looks like a prison with bars that separate various sections from each other. Even as a child I had to go through the sections by myself because they viewed me as an adult.

My first appointment gave me some hope. The doctor seemed

kind and as if he was listening to my story attentively. He looked at me with sincerity but also pity. He decided that it would be best for us to do X-rays, an ultrasound and some blood work, start physiotherapy and start on medication to help me function better. All my test results came back normal, leaving my doctor stumped at what could be causing my symptoms. In total I had to take 15 pills a day at the age of 14 to control what my doctor described as 'chronic back pain'. How many teenagers have chronic back pain issues? I still felt that something was wrong because my symptoms weren't solely isolated to my back. I had an array of other symptoms that he could not explain. I suffered from dizziness, nausea, intense headaches, heavy bleeding, excruciating menstrual cycles and constipation. My doctor ordered me to return in three months and every three months I would return to the same situation. I would go to bed early in the evening, my parents would wake me up at 4:30 am and I would get ready to leave by 5 am to get my clinic card in as early as possibly because there are no bookings. It is a first-come, first-served situation. In winter my dad would drop me off at my grandma's home nearby and start queueing outside the doors before it opened at 8 am.

The doors officially opened at 8 am but that was only really to process administrative tasks, like access your folder, have stickers printed, and allocate people to their designated doctor. The doctors would show up at around 10 am and begin seeing patients based on who was first, or who paid an admin clerk off to get them in above the rest. Naturally, a lot of unpleasantries and chaos ensued because people were all tired, frustrated, sick and just treated inadequately. People would shout at each other and call each other 'skelms' with 'blyn gedagtes' – which in Kaaps meant that they were sly people with ill intentions.

Waiting made me nervous. I felt out of place and stuck out in the crowd of older people like a sore thumb. Not many of my peers were regulars at the local clinic. It was an odd feeling because, on the one hand, you could feel the pity and the curiosity in people's eyes as they scanned my body – head to toe – looking for the obvious 'flaw' and coming up empty. On the other hand, some people were downright mean-spirited and would make snide remarks. Insinuating that I was looking for attention because I was young and looked 'fine'. They would be annoyed by the fact that I remained seated and didn't get up to stand and wait in line.

I recall the murmurs: 'I am telling you, Kieyah, today's children are not like our generation, they have no manners, they will remain sitting even though they can see an old person is standing.' My dad encouraged me to bring along earphones or a book, so I could zone out and ignore them. The truth was that those women who I reckon were probably around 60 years old were likely more able-bodied than I was. They could gleefully walk about the clinic from person to person they knew, chit-chatting, hand-on-the-hip, exclaiming 'hoelihaa!' when a story was particularly juicy. I, on the other hand, had difficulty climbing one flight of stairs and couldn't stand for long periods of time, and these symptoms only worsened. When eventually a patient left the doctor's room, we would all wait patiently, on the edge of our seats to bolt through the door lest we miss our call and get pushed down to the bottom of the patient pile for the day. When the doctor would call my name, and I entered the room, it felt like the air in the room dried up, like we both knew it was pointless to keep having three-month check-ups because we had done every test, every scan, every metric available to the clinic and nothing, absolutely nothing showed up on the tests.

The doctor looked at me like he was just about to give up. Tired of my case, he seemed distant and like he had completely run out of avenues to explore and yet my symptoms persisted. The doctor told me he thought we needed to change medication because the current pain medication regime wasn't working for me. He explained to me that I had to take the pain medication even if I didn't have pain at that particular time because I consistently needed the medication in my system to avoid the pain arising. I nodded along, staring past his head, to the window behind him and tried to swallow my tears and the lump in my throat. More medications, more pain killers, and no answers, no cure, no treatment, no clear cause of my symptoms. He told me that I had to start seeing him once a month instead of every third month because of my symptoms. He scribbled a date for a month from the day and asked me to have the admin clerk book the date for me. I thanked him and left the room with my brown paper medical folder with a yellow sticker on it identifying that I was a chronic patient but my case or symptoms were unclear. I walked up to the pharmacy section and proceeded to sit down with my folder until the clerk came out to fetch the next three rows of people – around 15 folders. A clerk told me I had to go by myself because of limited space – my dad wasn't allowed to sit with me. I tried hard to hold back my tears and the dread that came over me like an eclipse. I kept asking, 'What now? What next?' The pharmacy queue moved slowly as usual; there were not enough staff members to keep up with the hundreds of people showing up each day. Eventually a young woman came out and collected my folder. I sat and waited again for my name to be called over the intercom. I had to listen attentively because they would often call me 'Nadia' or mispronounce my last name as 'Dirkse'. Just as I suspected, the person over the intercom who spoke faster than Usain Bolt runs called for someone named 'Nadine Dirkse'. I got up and walked to the cracked glass window to receive my medication. I contemplated telling them that my name is Nadine Dirks, but what was the point? The entire system sets out to dehumanise people who need medical assistance. What is the point of arguing about my name each time? Next time, they will get it wrong again, I thought to myself, as I smiled and nodded when he asked if I was 'Nadine Dirkse'. The pharmacist handed me my one-month prescription of pain medication: 120 tablets of 500 g ibuprofen, 90 of 50 g tramadol, 240 of 500 g paracetamol. The pharmacist told me to take them daily as prescribed. In total, I was expected to take 15 painkillers per day. I vaguely listened as the pharmacist explained I was to take two paracetamol, one ibuprofen, one tramadol every morning, the same concoction at lunchtime and two paracetamol and one ibuprofen in the evening. Before bed I was instructed to take the same mixture of two paracetamol, one ibuprofen, one tramadol. I tried to keep track of what was being said but I kept thinking about side effects and addiction. I was only 15 years old and taking a fistful of painkillers a day – enough to put a horse to sleep, I'm sure.

The painkillers helped with my pain but didn't address the other issues I had. I was still bleeding heavily and even with the heavy pain medications, I could barely walk or see straight when menstruating. I still bled so severely that I would have to call my parents or sister at 3 in the morning because my bed sheets were drenched in blood. I was consistently bleeding massive chunks that resembled ox liver. On several occasions I would call my mother to examine my pads when I experienced the clots. I can't forget the fear in my mom's eyes. Her mouth contorted as if she was trying to shout but couldn't, she grabbed me and tried to help me get into the shower. My mother later told me that the only time she had seen a clot that resembled mine was when she had given birth to my sister and they had removed the afterbirth and shown it to her. She was in utter disbelief and couldn't understand how a clot could be that large. My mom insisted we ask the clinic for a referral to a tertiary hospital. Essentially the way the government healthcare system works is that you cannot just go to a hospital unless it is an emergency. You are meant to follow the system, which means visiting a GP for a referral to a community healthcare centre, and if they cannot assist at the clinic they should refer you to a tertiary hospital as a last resort. This process could take years, especially for a condition like mine which to doctors seemed inconvenient but not life-threatening. At my follow-up visits at the clinic, I had asked to be referred but the consensus was that I had to try everything they had to offer first. The doctor then prescribed the same medication but this time around added more tramadol and suggested I try physiotherapy and a hormonal contraceptive. I attended a few sessions with the physiotherapist, all of which proved to be of no help because I had no clinical diagnosis to base the treatment plan on. She suggested, to help with pain, I try sleeping with a pillow between my legs. The hormonal contraceptive pill, which I was supposed to take continuously on a loop and skip the inert doses to keep my period away didn't work. I still managed to get my period. I bleed through the two-month hormonal contraceptive injection as well, and it gave me blinding headaches. I couldn't take the medication because it made me drowsy to the point of sedation and I had to take public transport to and from school. Being semi-sedated in a taxi as a teenage girl in South Africa is a horror story waiting to happen. I decided to skip the medications and live with the pain in favour of school and functioning. We switched to the three-month hormonal injection, which seemed to keep my period away at least. Even then the other symptoms persisted but I had to accept it. I eventually opted out of seeing the doctor at the clinic when I was around 16 because it was the same old. The doctor had got to the point of not even examining me, to just giving me a script for medication during our consults. I decided it would be less time-consuming and anxiety-inducing to go to a place where I felt I wasn't being heard or taken seriously.

I maintained the hormonal contraceptive injections for another year, but my symptoms only worsened. I started experiencing intense abdominal pain, constant lower back pain, persistent constipation, dizziness, headaches, bloating and nausea. It was difficult doing physical activities. I fell off the entire healthcare system and stopped getting the injections altogether because it felt pointless and ridiculous to continue when my symptoms hadn't cleared up. No one had any answers, no one cared to follow up or to refer me to someone who may have been more equipped to handle my symptoms and case.

In July 2014, I had just turned 19 three months prior, but the same symptoms persisted and I felt as if the lower right side of my abdomen was swollen. I recall it being a very cold and overcast day, as I showed my mom my abdomen to see if it was swollen. She remarked that it did look swollen compared to the left side. She fixed me a hot water bottle, gave me two paracetamols and told me to keep warm to help with the pain. She told me GPs were likely closed because it was a Sunday evening and suggested that if the issue doesn't resolve by the next day, she would take me to the GP.

The symptoms persisted and I still felt swollen the next morning. My mom took me to our local GP who examined me thoroughly and agreed that my abdomen was distended but reminded us it could be many things. He asked me for a urine sample to test in his office so he could establish what it could be. The doctor looked at my mom and me over the rim of his glasses and said, 'I am going to write you a referral to the hospital immediately. You have to go immediately.' I looked at my mom for assurance and she asked him what the issue was. He said in no uncertain terms that something was very wrong, that we had to look at the possibility that I was suffering from appendicitis. He told us there was blood in my urine, nitrites marking infection and leucocytes, which indicated that my body had been fighting some kind of an infection for some time.

The gravity of the situation didn't hit us until I asked where I should wait for my medication. That is when he said he couldn't treat it with oral medication and that I needed to go to the hospital immediately.

Prejudice, cut me open

I SUPPOSE IT IS JUST THE nature of people to look at someone and attempt to categorise them to figure out how to treat them. I don't think we examine just how egregious that truly is. We do it with disabilities, race, ethnicity, religions, gender, sexuality and physical health. You name it; we would find a way to categorise it. Identifiers are important but not when they are used to actively harm individuals, and that is exactly what my experience has been. People have always looked at me and assigned labels to me and denied my basic human rights based on the categories in their heads. Socialisation causes us to walk around judging and labelling based on our internal prejudices without ever stepping back to think: 'Is this how I actually feel or think? Or are my prejudices and biases kicking in?' I would love to assume we live in a world where people have that level of self-awareness but it's simply not the reality. You would think people who serve their communities are a little bit more self-aware and keep their biases in check, but that, too, is a fantasy.

As a young person reliant on the public healthcare system, I naively believed in doctors and believed that they were somehow more evolved than other humans – that they don't act on their prejudices – but I quickly saw the reality in how doctors treated me and abused me in many ways. I could feel their disdain in their coldness towards me, never quite engaging with me as if I were a person. They would scribble notes and sigh as I described what I was experiencing; they dismissed my complaints and implied that 'You're a young girl, you look fine. Periods are painful, you need to take Panado.' The same kind of dismissal worsened as I aged because then, even as a teenage girl, white supremacy sees Black children as adults, and they will treat you like one in an attempt to further harm, abuse and break down girls who are already vulnerable, scared and unable to defend themselves.

It was overcast and chilly as we arrived at the hospital with the letter from my GP. I was holding my mom's arm to steady myself as I walked. The hospital's ugly mint green walls and metal benches seemed fuzzy, like it was a blur but moving at the same time. My mom led me to the reception area and sat me down in a chair in front of the admin clerk. My mom's voice was shaky and strained as she urged, 'My daughter is sick... I was sent here, I don't know where to go or what to do first. She's in severe pain and bleeding heavily. Where do we go?' I don't remember the clerk; I tried to keep my head down to keep the dizziness at bay. She smashed the keys on her keypad and printed out stickers with my details and handed us a folder, gesturing to where we needed to wait. My mom helped me up from the worn, generic blue upholstered chair, and led me to the waiting area. She sat me down on the hard metal bench in the waiting area and wrapped a small scarf over my legs to keep me warm.

'Askies, meisie, I should have brought you a blanket, it's cold but I was in a rush. I'm going to hand in your folder, stay here, I'm coming back, ne?'

Weak, I raised my head to smile slightly, assuring her I was okay, and she walked towards the nurses' station at the emergency room. The doors were closed and a harsh-looking security guard stood at the entrance allowing one person in at a time to hand the folder to the nurse, which was usually slotted in at the very bottom to keep a sense of order as to who arrived first. We waited, and waited, and waited. I leaned my head onto my mom's arm, falling asleep and waking up periodically. I distinctly recall feeling very cold, hungry and tired, and the pain was absolutely blinding. Eventually, a stocky nurse, with short, crimson-dyed hair, Crocs and glasses came out and called my name so that she could triage me. Essentially, it is a system to categorise people in order of how serious their condition is. It is a flawed system because blood pressure, blood sugar levels, temperature and weight checks can only tell so much. The nurses rely on how well patients can perform their illness to be seen by a doctor with haste. I didn't realise this. Generally, I am a quiet sick person. I generally don't make a sound and remain very still, so the nurse took that to mean I was well enough to be categorised as 'green' which means non-emergency. They tend to 'red' and then 'orange/yellow' patients first and then green. Public hospitals could be an excellent place to scout for future Oscar-award-winning actors. People flung themselves to the ground, writhing in 'severe' pain, kicking and screaming hysterically, begging God to take them and alleviate their suffering. I watched in horror, wondering what was happening. These people were usually seen first by doctors because of their performances only to be sent home five minutes after being examined with some paracetamol. Nurses would passive aggressively comment on how people waste public resources, time and efforts when they are not sick and are just 'sitting aan vir aandag', evidently just looking for attention. Once a red-haired nurse responded by saying, 'I knew it… I have never seen someone in severe pain able to throw themselves onto the floor.' Yet, these people still got preference because until you examine them, how do you determine who is actually on their deathbed and who just wanted to hang out at the hospital on a weeknight?

I was terrified, sick and in severe pain and was told that I am grown up and had to go through the doors to the emergency side by myself. As if adults don't require emotional or physical support. I fought back my tears as I walked in by myself without my mom, completely unaware of what was going to happen and what was wrong with me. All I wanted was to hold my mom's hand and not fear for my safety. The room I was sent to held at least 50 patients – all with varying degrees of emergencies. Some had been stabbed and were bleeding through their torn shirts. Some were in active labour with a look of terror on their faces. An older man was asked to wear a mask and told to keep it on and not cough close to people but he refused. Several women had babies who were screaming bloody murder in discomfort. A young man with a fade and in a wheelchair had gunshot wounds and he was crying in pain, begging for nurses to give him pain medication, in between screaming 'Allah'. Two women walked in with thick blankets – you know the kind with the Big Five on it – wailing about unspecified pain. I distinctively remember someone gasping for air, with a clearly tight chest. I sat there observing everyone, terrified that someone would die before they were attended to. The room was dark with only one light, everyone looked afraid and tired. We waited for what seemed like a lifetime, with no doctor in sight. Eventually a doctor showed up, seeing a patient every 30–45 minutes. Finally, the group thinned out, some people got impatient and left, some were transferred elsewhere, and the rest of us remained in the freezing, drafty dark room.

I was shivering and my hands were so cold they started to take on a grey hue. I got out my cell phone which I had not wanted to use because my battery was on 20%. I thought about how ill-prepared I was and wished I had known I would be sitting at the hospital in the early hours of the morning, freezing, hungry, scared and alone, with a phone that would die in the next few hours. It seemed like there was a lull and people were not being called in any longer, I checked my phone and it was nearly 3 am. I had been there for nine hours straight. My mom had been sending me WhatsApp messages to assure me she was right outside and kept checking in. I felt defeated. I had been in excruciating pain for days: I couldn't walk without assistance and my lower back felt as though someone had repeatedly kicked me. My right abdominal area was swollen, tender and especially painful. I just wanted to go home and get into my warm bed. I was exhausted and the cold made my pain much worse. I sent my mom a WhatsApp: 'I want to go home, I am tired, I can't do this. I would rather be sick at home, I'm in too much pain, Mommy.' My mom responded and said okay, and I heard her voice demanding they let me leave because I was not getting any assistance and I was worsening. My mom told the nurse I was in a ridiculous amount of pain and sitting in the cold waiting for hours isn't helping me. The nurse came to me and explained that the beds in the emergency room were all full and we needed to wait for one before a doctor could see to me. She handed me a Styrofoam cup with some room temperature water and one tramadol and two paracetamols. A young man in the corner, with a bloody torn T-shirt in a wheelchair, shouted at the nurse, 'I've also been here waiting and in pain. Why do some people get special treatment?' The nurse turned to him with her hands on her hips and said, 'Well, some people have God-given ailments and some want to be gangsters and get shot. As jy nie hoor nie dan moen jy voel.' I was taken aback by her lack of empathy and disregard for his pain based on his history. How could a nurse tell someone to suffer because of their wrongdoing? Shouldn't nurses be compassionate to all patients?

The nurse went back to tell my mom that she had given me pain medication and urged my mother not to take me home. I heard her tell my mom: 'Ma'am, we can't let you leave with her because her doctor picked up something is wrong and sent her here. If she goes, you must sign a form to say we aren't liable if something happens to her. I will go check for a bed.'

My mom was infuriated because she felt that during the long wait for assistance, I could have become worse and so either way they had not done anything to help me. The nurse came back quickly with a wheelchair to take me to the emergency room where a bed had miraculously appeared. My mom still wasn't allowed to come inside with me but at least I was going to be examined by a doctor. The doctor assigned to me was a young, blonde woman who seemed kind. She looked at the note from my doctor, asked me a series of questions and began doing tests – ranging from urine samples to blood tests, and arranged for an X-ray to be done. While the doctor was on a call to arrange my X-ray, I started to feel really hot all of sudden and like I was sweating bullets. I felt the wave of nausea hit me. I tried to get myself off the bed, so I could try and throw up in the bathroom but I was so dizzy and couldn't get off the bed myself. I tried to call for help but instead I projectile vomited all over the bed before I could even try and aim for the floor.

I waited to be taken for X-rays while a nurse helped clean me up. I overheard the doctor discuss my symptoms with the other doctors in the room, all of whom glanced over at me while she explained my case. I overheard them conclude, 'She has symptoms of appendicitis. We have to treat it immediately.' My X-ray results were clear and showed no issues. I was then sent for an abdominal ultrasound, which ruled out the appendicitis concern but did show that I had a vascular mass on an ovary that was 4x4 cm big. The doctors told me I would need to be taken to the Obstetrics and Gynaecology (Obs & Gynae) ward because of the location of the mass, and I was not allowed to eat because I may need to have surgery. I nodded in agreement but I don't believe I fully grasped what was being said to me at the time. I was just thankful that someone seemed to listen to me and there was some kind of progress in terms of tests and findings. I wasn't imagining my symptoms, I wasn't overreacting – it was validating albeit scary and unpleasant. By the time I was wheeled to the Obs & Gynae ward the sun was out and the hospital had come alive again.

I was met by a young, male gynae who had been assigned to my case. He was tall, white and smug. He pulled the curtains closed and started to interrogate me in a ward full of women. I was stunned and confused about what he was saying and why he was being so vicious.

He said to me, 'You people always get botched abortions, and then you come in here bleeding and in pain afterwards.'

I looked at him grinning at me like my suffering was somehow amusing to him and I said, 'Abortion? What abortion?'

He laughed and said in a snarky tone, 'Don't play dumb, don't lie, because I'm going to examine you and find out anyway, so you may as well just be honest.'

I started to hyperventilate, my face felt hot and I tried not to cry but I couldn't contain myself. I tried to speak in between sobs and tried to tell him that I was being honest.

He smirked and said, 'We'll see.'

I asked for my mom and he told me that my mom wasn't allowed to be present with me. He disappeared behind the curtain and I sobbed relentlessly, paralysed by the experience and confused as to why the doctor not only didn't believe me but also seemed to get some sort of pleasure out of my suffering. I prayed silently that he would leave me alone given he thought I was lying, but soon after, he came back with a metal trolley with medical tools that looked like medieval torture devices in his hands. Little did I know this would be the beginning of medical procedures being used to punish me for existing in the body I exist in – racism, misogynoir and bias towards me; abuse, neglect and mistreatment towards my body.

I remember a sharp, stabbing and burning pain as the doctor jammed the speculum into my body. He didn't do it gently, he didn't coach me through it, and he chose the biggest one he could find with the intention of harming me. I cried and instinctively tried to force my legs shut. He tried to hold my leg while calling for a nurse to hold my other leg down so he could open the speculum. I gasped for air, forgetting how to breathe because of the blinding pain and panic. It felt like an eternity and he told me to relax because I was making it harder on myself by panicking.

'Me? I was making it worse?' I thought to myself.

I don't remember what else he did, which I suspect has to be my mind's way of protecting me from the horror of what I had experienced. It felt as if I blacked out because I don't recall him finishing the examination and leaving, I just remember the ceiling – it looked like it was made out of papier mâché. The texture looked rough and uneven, differing from square to square. I felt someone rubbing my arm and looked down and saw the nurse. She was checking in on me and set up an intravenous drip so that she could give me antibiotics, pain medication and fluids to keep me hydrated.

I must have fallen asleep because when I woke up the sun was blazing in through the window. My mom was sitting by my bedside watching me attentively. A tall, brunette woman wearing purple scrubs came to introduce herself to us as my surgeon.

She explained, 'We need to do emergency surgery to remove a mass on your right ovary. Unfortunately, we may have to remove the entire ovary depending on the damage. Do you understand?'

I nodded and repeated what she said and asked her, 'Why do I need surgery? What is it?'

She looked at me sympathetically and told me. 'To be honest, we don't know. It is vascular, so it is different to a cyst. We will have to operate in order to determine the cause.'

I was scared to death. I had never had surgery before, but I understood the need for it. I was grateful I had a different surgeon and looked over at my mom who was frowning and concerned. My mother looked as if she had aged ten years over the course of the night. My mom's voice broke as she asked the surgeon, 'How long will the surgery be? What will you do? Cut her?'

She answered flatly: 'I'm sorry, yes, we will have to cut her. It will be a laparotomy and the aim is to remove the mass so we anticipate 45 minutes.'

I signed the paperwork and began to prepare for the surgery, taking off my grandmother's ring, removing my underwear, leaving my glasses behind. I was able to see my father and my sister before being taken to the operating rooms. My sister and father said very little and seemed sombre. My sister must have sensed my fear when she piped up enthusiastically that it would be fast, and 'we will be right outside, waiting for you when you come out'. I felt a lump in my throat, and I knew if I tried to speak I would expose the terror I felt; I needed to be brave for my family. As I was wheeled to theatre, with my parents and sister accompanying me, I started to cry silently, betraying myself and my bravery. I said goodbye and as the porters wheeled me in, I started to think about how my parents would react if I didn't survive the surgery. The thought made my body feel completely lame.

I woke up in the recovery room to loud talking and bright lights. I felt groggy and confused about where I was. I felt the pain in my abdomen; it was dull, radiating and hot. I tried to locate the loud talking. It was coming from my right, a nurse talking to another nurse on the other side of the room. She noticed I had woken up and her eyes lit up as she smiled and said: 'There you go! How do you feel? Are you okay? You are finished now, you can go back to the ward.'

I groaned in agony; my belly felt like it had been ripped apart by a chainsaw. The nurse called a porter to take me back to the ward. As we neared the ward, I saw my family: pacing, head in hands, my mom on the phone hysterical. They rushed to me and asked how I was doing. My surgery had gone on for nearly three hours instead of the 45 minutes they were expecting and no one had informed my family.

Groggy from anaesthesia and pain, I fell in and out of sleep once I was back in the Obs & Gynae ward. My surgeon came by to check on me. She explained that my surgery went on for longer than expected. She looked haggard and told me, 'No one could have prepared me for what I saw when I opened you up. It's not just the mass. You have adhesions and masses all over your ovaries, uterus, fallopian tubes.' She paused and said, 'Your fallopian tubes were behind your uterus and attached to your bowels which it pulled down. I've sent it away for further tests but I think you may have really severe endometriosis.'

When I asked her if she was able to remove it all, she looked at me with pity and said, 'No, I don't have the expertise. I removed what I could; it's permanent. You can't permanently remove endometriosis.'

I tried to focus and absorb what she was saying but suddenly everything made sense, all those years of suffering all added up. I caught bits of what she was saying in between my racing thoughts and my life and my future. She said, 'This may cause infertility, especially because yours is so severe.'

My abdomen had thirty-something staples holding it together and searing pain completely eviscerating any hope of getting up and going home. God, I thought to myself, what else could go wrong?

The following day I got an unexpected and unpleasant visitor – the cruel doctor who had violently examined me. He smirked and for a split second I thought, 'Maybe he'll apologise for being so wicked.' I was wrong.

'Endometriosis, huh?' and chuckled. 'I didn't even consider it. Europeans mostly get endometriosis; I didn't even consider that *you* could have endometriosis.' He shook his head in disbelief and left. No apology.

The strange reality of getting a life-altering diagnosis in a state facility is the coldness. No one seems to have the time to sit with their patients and talk to them, they don't refer you to a therapist or provide any support in the way of psychological care. They give you the facts very bluntly and move to the next patient. My diagnosis took a major toll on me and what I thought my life would be. Suddenly I had a lifelong label attached to me that would inhibit me from doing all the things I had planned for in my life. In a few hours everything I knew was over and gone, and I had to suck it up and keep it together, push it under the carpet. My surgeon came by during her rounds to check my folder and hear how I was doing. She explained the extent of the endometriosis again. I suppose she felt the need to reiterate considering I had been in a haze the day before. She said very explicitly that it would be very unlikely that I would be able to conceive; she didn't sugarcoat it. I just gazed ahead, with a lump in my throat, seeing flashes in my mind's eye of the life I could have had with children and a nuclear family being snatched away from me. I hadn't really considered having children at that point in my life; it wasn't a well-thought-out plan but the reality of the choice being taken from me dawned on me.

'You are very unlikely to conceive.' Just like that, my life, limited and altered without my input.

The conception conversation was a catalyst for a deeper issue that I hadn't yet thought of in my hospital bed. My life would never be the same, every plan I had for myself, my career and my future wouldn't materialise, I wouldn't be able to do what my peers do, I wouldn't be able to pursue a career that required me to be physically active. All my hard work and plans to pursue becoming a medical doctor, or a nature conservationist or a chef simply wouldn't work with severe chronic pain. My symptoms worsen when I need to be active and all the paths I had worked towards required me to be on the go, on my feet and quick on my toes. Reality hit me like a train on the tracks, I couldn't do what I had dreamed about…

'What am I going to do now? Where do I go from here? I'm stuck.' Stuck in my bed, stuck on the Cape Flats, stuck in my parents' home, stuck in a loop of dependency on others for my survival. I hate being a liability, I want to be free, I want to stand on my own feet. I must have disassociated or passed out because when I opened my eyes, the doctor had left and the sky started to quickly turn from light grey to a deep smoky grey. The blue sky turning grey matched the way I felt inside – heavy, dark and gloomy.

The thoughts of my life being over before it even started dawned on me, the feeling of overwhelm washed over me and clutched my body in a tight, suffocating hug. I cried and cried until I couldn't catch my breath. With each sob rippling through my body, my incision responded with a searing pain. I tried to slow my breathing to keep from panicking even more; I felt a hand on my arm comforting me. I looked to my right and realised that the woman in the bed next to me had gotten out of her bed to try and comfort me. She wiped my tears with the back of her hand and gently rubbed on my arm whispering 'Phephisa, sisi ... it's okay, it's okay, it's okay. Don't worry.' I cried into the arms of a stranger who through her own medical issues showed me compassion that can never be repaid. I told her how my life would never be the same, the idea of normalcy no longer existed for me. I leaned in and said, 'In my community, people expect you to get married and have children. No one marries the barren women, because there is no point or status attached.' The internalised misogyny and pain of my childhood spewed from my lips. I couldn't believe it because that's not who I am, I don't care about the male gaze and fulfilling an archaic womanly role, but I knew that for the rest of my life that's how my community would view me: a barren woman with nothing to offer.

I would be viewed with the perception that a woman's duty is to get married, take care of her husband and have children and if I couldn't do that then I had no value, nothing to offer and was simply useless. The sad reality is that the world views women as valuable for what they can offer with their bodies and labour – it is all physical. I didn't want to be viewed that way and I didn't want to internalise ridiculous ideals. No one ever asked me how I really am; they would ask me so they could ask about my reproductive abilities and pity me because my womb is defective. The questions are always: 'How are you, how's your health? So ... what are the doctors saying, how are you going to have children?'

I answer these questions the same way each time in a flat tone, 'I'm okay. I don't know, it seems unlikely that I can have children.' Their faces dropping, lips downturned, with a look of pity in their eyes. People seem to mourn my illness and ability to procreate more than I do. It is the strangest projection I have ever witnessed. They don't ask me if I'm sad or what I wanted, they just assume my feelings would align with theirs. The reality is that it is just that important to some people and they seek out people who are able to procreate. It is an unspoken requirement. People date with the intention of forming a bond with someone – and to have children. There is no room for people who can't fulfil the need. I pity women who don't know they have reproductive issues until they start to procreate because the rejection, shaming and blaming that women endure at the hands of their husbands, families and communities for not procreating is indescribable.

The treatment in public healthcare facilities is bound to turn anyone into some kind of activist. The overall disregard for some patients over others is jarring. The same kind of stigma you experience in the outside world is what even healthcare professionals treat patients with. The kind woman who had comforted me was discharged the following day and within a few hours her bed was occupied by a different woman. She spoke with a thick accent I couldn't place and wrapped herself in her purple gown. She seemed to spend a lot of her time reading her Bible. I observed her and her husband coming to see her and wondered if she missed home. Later that evening she disclosed to me that she was in hospital because she was pregnant and had a hernia in her pelvic region, so they were keeping her to monitor her and ensure a safe pregnancy. She seemed worried that she may need surgery if her symptoms didn't ease up because of where the baby was situated and growing. We kept each other company, and when I told her that I had just had surgery for endometriosis and I was recovering, she looked at me with care and concern and reminded me of the strength of the women in the Bible. She shared with me that she was actually from Uganda and missing her family terribly but came to South Africa for opportunities with her husband and two children. She shared photos and I shared my snacks with her. Unexpectedly one of the doctors stopped by with a scowl on her face. She stopped at the woman's bed and without warning pulled the curtains shut around her bed. I have no idea as to whether the doctor assumed because she cannot see me that I cannot hear her. Without an ounce of gentleness or care for the woman's state of mind she spoke loud enough for me to hear. 'Do you know that you have HIV?' she said in an accusatory tone, and before my friend could even answer her, she bombarded her with more questions, urging her to call her husband, to test her children, asking about her sexual partners and if she knew how damaging it was to the baby. She accused her as if she knew and simply didn't care. My friend's voice became muffled and strained. She repeatedly said: 'HIV? HIV? How? Are you sure?' I resented the fact that the doctor handled the news in such a callous and accusatory manner but most of all, I loathed the stigma and discrimination that dripped from each question she gunned down without awaiting a response. The doctor seemed to get frustrated with the woman and didn't offer her any opportunity to speak or discuss her feelings and a way forward. She got up abruptly, aggressively flung the curtains open and stormed off. My friend sat in her bed, in her purple gown, motionless, blank. I struggled my way up, using a towel to hold my stapled belly together and headed over to her, closing the curtain the doctor had flung open. I handed her a tissue and said it was okay to collect herself before we opened the curtains. The woman wailed and asked what she had done wrong in her lifetime to deserve this, she said to me she is sure I heard everything and so she didn't need to hide. I held her hand and nodded, fighting the lump in my throat. She calmed down enough to say to me that she had never had a sexual partner before her husband and that she couldn't understand how it could be.

The sheer discrimination towards people with STDs and STIs in public healthcare is startling and one of many reasons for the work I do. Today I work in advocacy because I have seen the discrimination women face intimately. I spent the evening counselling my new friend, sharing information, success stories, statistics, and every factual piece of information I had gathered in my HIV/AIDS advocacy work. Although I was only 19, I had been trained as a counsellor to break down the stigma of HIV/AIDS through my voluntary work. I answered her questions as best as I could and tried to soothe her fears. I spent the next few days in the role of a counsellor because I couldn't turn a blind eye to the mistreatment of Black women and the vile assumptions made. Healthcare should be the one place people feel safe enough to test positive for an STD or STI, but it isn't the reality. So many healthcare professionals use STD and STI results as a measurement of morals and therefore how they are entitled to treat you based on your results or reason for being in hospital.

No one came to speak to the woman next to me, to counsel her, to soothe her anxiety. No one came to tell her what her options and next steps were. They left her alone, afraid and anxious. I counselled her, spoke to her about people I knew who were thriving while being HIV+, how new medications were available. I tried to encourage her. The stigma in these hospitals is absolutely mind blowing. As I lay in my hospital bed, waiting for the next thirty minutes to pass so that I could get my next dose of painkillers post-surgery, I tried to lie very still and focus my eyes on the ceiling to keep from focusing on the hot pain that travelled across my abdomen. I closed my eyes and tried to keep my breath steady and calm, but I felt myself becoming hot and flustered. The pain just intensified rapidly and I found myself shouting for a nurse before I could even think about what I would ask. Only later in my journey would I learn that those bells to call for help in hospitals aren't just in movies – you just don't find them in public hospitals. I guess it's one of those things, if you can't call, then you must be okay and if you're not, well, they're understaffed. The nurse showed up at my side and asked me what was wrong. I tried to steady my voice to keep from crying because of the level of pain I was in. She told me that they were preparing to do their next medication round and I would have to wait just a few minutes because the senior nurse had to go get the morphine from some locked room. I swallowed the lump in my throat, nodded and tried to half smile at the nurse as she patted my hand. Another woman in the ward, who looked like she could be in her mid-twenties or so, with curly dark hair exclaimed that she was in pain too and needed to be given pain medication as soon as possible. The nurse looked up at her and scoffed loudly, saying, 'Ja, ja, you will have to be patient ... we are getting the medication. In any case, don't cry now, you brought this on yourself.' I looked at the nurse and at the woman who looked stunned at what she was hearing. She repeated her initial request for pain medication and the nurse in a mean-spirited tone told her that she didn't ask for pain medication when she was sleeping around. She said, 'As julle nie wil hoor nie, dan moet julle voel!' In short: there are consequences to one's actions. I was lost as to what was happening and why the nurse had suddenly changed her tone from kind and accommodating to me, and vicious and mean to the other woman who had asked the same thing I did. Soon after, an older nurse with a serious face, thick glasses and additional lapels indicating a higher nursing rank walked in with the silver medicine cart.

Although my bed was at the very end of the ward by the window the nurse who had just comforted me and told me the medication was on its way headed over to the serious-faced nurse and motioned to me, and side eyed the other woman asking for medication. The two nurses headed over to me, looked at my file and made a few notes before preparing a needle to give me morphine and added a few pills to a little cup for me to have too. They spoke loudly about how they would make the other woman wait longer and tend to me, and others first, because we had God-given illnesses and not vuil siek (an STD/STI). They thought it was appropriate for her to feel the pain and suffering as a punishment. My mind was absolutely blown. I was in no position myself to stand up for her, even though I knew it was wrong and that it shouldn't matter what's ailing her. I knew if I had said anything I would be subjected to the same kind of bullying. I looked at her apologetically, and turned away so they could inject the morphine into my arm.

I started university the following year and had to figure out how to manage life as a chronically ill girl from the Cape Flats. It was a living nightmare; I bled daily and would get dizzy because of the constant loss of blood. I tried to walk to the bus stop every day with people I knew in case my body gave out and I fainted along the way. It was terrifying thinking that I could potentially pass out while alone in the middle of the Cape Town central business district. My legs would ache as if my body was too heavy for my feet to carry me. Everything just seemed so much harder to do – even simple things like climbing the stairs. The endometriosis fatigue made my eyelids feel like heavy rocks threatening to roll down and shut my eyes in the middle of lectures. The pain continued and kept me off on the occasional day. Adjusting to my life with endometriosis was exceptionally difficult, it impacted every part of my life and who I was.

When you're young and chronically ill, everyone assumes you're well because you're young and you don't look sick. I don't fully understand what people want chronically ill people to look like but that's the general consensus: people should look sick. The assumption that young people are fit and healthy, mixed in with good old-fashioned African values about respecting your elders is a hell of a mixture. When you take public transport, it is an unspoken rule that younger people get up and offer their seat to someone who is elderly, disabled or pregnant. After waiting in a long line that snaked around the bus terminus, I got in and the driver clipped my clipcard and I chose to sit on the blue two-seater by the window. An older woman walked by and stopped next to me asking me, 'Is it okay if I sit here?' I said sure. The bus started to fill up and we moved through traffic rather slowly. As we approached a bus stop, I spotted a woman who looked like she could be in her late fifties running for the bus.

She ran and dragged on her cigarette harshly to finish her smoke before getting onto the packed bus. The woman walked in and looked at me as if waiting for me to get up and I averted eye contact and looked outside the window to watch the cars slowly trickle by. The woman loudly started to drop hints in a passive aggressive tirade about how the youth are rude and disrespectful. 'When I was young, we would always get up and allow the older people to sit down. Kids of today are disrespectful and they have no manners.'

I knew she was talking to me but I ignored her, thinking to myself, 'I just saw this woman run after a bus while smoking and she expects me to get up? I can't even walk fast without triggering my pain, how can I get up and allow her to sit based on age when I would likely pass out from pain if I were to stand the whole way home.' She looked at me and assumed based on how I looked that I must be fit and healthy and that needs to change because it is ridiculous to look at people and attempt to dissect their health.

The reality is my life changed forever in ways I never thought it would, and I had to suck it up and keep going. No one sat down and spoke to me about the life I had and the future I wanted and showed me how to mourn those elements of myself. My body, my mind and my future fell apart and I had to cry on the inside because I didn't want to make anyone uncomfortable. I didn't want to see the hurt in my parents' eyes, I didn't want to burden my friends. I had to understand that in all honesty no one would truly be able to comprehend what I was going through and they couldn't really help me because they didn't have the tools or experience. It was a challenge trying to explain to people why I couldn't keep up with them and I hated feeling different, like an outsider.

My friends couldn't begin to imagine what my life was like, and how different our experiences were. I watched them running around carefree, going out, going to bars and clubs, going on hiking trips and I couldn't participate. It is hard to accept that by 4 pm after a day of lectures, I was nearly catatonic and my peers could walk from Woodstock to Long Street to go out clubbing. I would sit and listen to their stories and look at photos the next day, pretending to be unbothered and excited for them but internally I felt like I was broken and defective. I would think. 'Why can't you just be normal and suck it up? Why can't you just push through for once' and I tried hard because I wanted to maintain my friendships with my peers but it just wasn't possible. How do you explain to your 21-year-old friends who are stumbling in their platform heels and cute outfits that you don't feel well and that we need to leave when their crushes have just asked them to dance, when they've ordered another round of drinks in a dark, stuffy club the size of a shoebox, or when their favourite song just came on?

Life with a chronic illness is unkind, unfair and alienating but, being older, I can say without a doubt, it is much easier as you age and the absolute worst as someone in their late teens to early twenties. People in those age groups haven't lived much or experienced much and they can be self-involved even when they mean well. They don't really make accommodations for disabled or chronically ill people and, as someone in that age group, you don't consider asking because you don't know anything else either. When you're a young adult, especially in the South African context, there isn't much else modelled to us as alternative ways to have fun. All we know is drinking, clubbing and parties. No one really talks about picnics, spa days, lunch or dinner dates, or anything remotely accommodating and I get why – it is an accessibility issue. How many young Black and Brown kids can afford to do dinner dates with a friend? It requires transportation to and from the restaurant and money for a meal, a drink and a tip. It is way cheaper to get 15 people together at one person's home, each with R100, and buy some stuff to braai and spend the rest on alcohol. It changes as we age because we have more experiences, access and more financial freedom. I also found it a lot easier to assert myself and ask friends to do things I am able to do because I know that at this age in our lives I wouldn't be putting them in an awkward predicament.

Some experiences got easier for me and some became harder and some were entirely new to me. Dating as a young person who is chronically ill or disabled is dehumanising. People don't consider us worthy to date and make it clear that it is an issue for them. People are bold enough to look you in the face and tell you, 'I could never date you… you can't have children'. It never stops shocking me because, aside from it being discrimination, the entitlement from able-bodied people is astounding. The fact that people instinctively think because someone is differently abled that we have any desire to make them a life partner is comical. I doubt someone would utter those words to a healthy, able-bodied person but, when you're not, you must just be waiting by the door like a dog hoping someone will choose you. I feel as if I evaporate from my body and view those kinds of scenes from above, looking down at the ridiculousness and thinking to myself, 'Personally, who would want to have a child with an entitled, selfish, ableist fool?' I don't say it, but I am sure the laugh that escapes my lips for a millisecond tells on me. The part that makes me cringe and laugh most of all is that those types of people are usually deadbeat parents, absent or otherwise not really interested in being one. They only demand the ability from women because society says they have to, because it is what proves their manhood and virility to the world. I would hate to be a child that my father insisted on and yet has no interest in actually parenting me. The question to these types is simple: 'Aren't you embarrassed?'

I don't think we are ever taught to evaluate what we want, I don't think I have ever experienced it in my own life or the lives around me. Maybe my community is an outlier but how many people are encouraged to think about what they want? Hell, how many people are encouraged to think? If we were encouraged to think about what we want, I wonder how many people would be married, how many would have children, how many would keep their unwanted pregnancies, how many would be in relationships with the opposite sex? I don't think we ever ask those questions and so we go through life chasing what we think we should be instead of what we want. It builds resentment, too. I know many women who are moms and claim they love it but get genuinely mad at women who don't have children and accuse them of being selfish and lazy. I have heard moms say that women without children aren't real women and that they're not really happy, but I suspect it is a lot of projection on the part of moms who feel like they didn't have a choice. I think that the same society that pressures women to be married to a man and bear children also makes it so that moms have to be superhuman. They can't express frustration, they can't have a life outside of their families, they can't talk about how hard it is and how they wish they were childfree and single. If they do they're considered bad moms, as if they aren't human, no matter how much you love something or someone. Sometimes it gets frustrating and that's okay.

Those same societal standards and projections are then transferred onto other vulnerable groups of people, like chronically ill and disabled women. People don't see us as individuals, they see us as defective, and then they immediately consider our 'defect' through a normative lens. I can't begin to count how many times I've met someone new and their immediate response after hearing about my condition is: 'Oh no, I'm so sorry, that's so sad... So, what about children and a husband?' Suddenly the buzzing room of people quietens down and it feels like hot rays coming from their eyes are piercing into me. Now I have to sit there and answer Susan, my neighbour's daughter's transport lady's questions about my health and life. I really want to tell her to F-off but I can't. I just grin and keep the answers short. 'It's not sad. I don't know if I want to get married or have children.' The response to my answer depends. Some people try to change my mind and some think I am saying it because I am feeling insecure about it. I would much rather have people ask me about how it affects me, or how it affects work or what I enjoy doing rather than imposing their strange views and desires onto me. Better yet, I wish people, particularly those we don't know, would stop asking chronically ill and disabled people about our medical histories at a party. Now that would be my idea of an ideal future.

All my life, I had to fight

THE SOUTH AFRICAN CONTEXT of a faulty public healthcare system, apartheid spatial planning, class and race divides breeds a strange state of being. Either we endure suffering silently, escaping into another world in order to survive the torment or we advocate for ourselves and others. Both of these methods form from a sense of helplessness and self-preservation – it is a case of do or die. My experiences of the public healthcare system as a young girl in the townships forced me into advocacy early in my teens because I watched healthcare providers disregard and mistreat people who they deemed guilty of causing their own suffering. I watched nurses separate patients into categories: people with HIV or AIDS and the others. They would make no secret about the reason for the discrimination; they would stand in front of the crowd and almost gleefully remark that the right section was for 'AIDS patients'. The stocky, middle-aged passive aggressive nurse would go on to let the crowd know that these patients needed to see the two doctors available to them to help with their AIDS. They disclosed people's medical information if they thought it was due to immoral behaviour. That's just how it was – no one said anything besides murmuring about how rude the nurses were. The group on the right would look down at the floor; I imagine they must have wanted the ground to open up and swallow them in that moment. I would cringe at the audacity until I just couldn't control myself and would loudly ask the nurses why they felt the need to humiliate people and disclose their medical history. I demanded to know why they singled out certain patients and if they realised that they were doing more harm than good because who would want to get tested or come in for check-ups and medication if they knew they would face abuse?

The passive aggressive nurse had turned and scowled at me, and her colleague, whose voice sounded like she had been born with a built-in megaphone, started to remind me about who was in charge. The room suddenly came to a hush; you could hear the sound of people holding their breaths and I could feel their eyes on me. This is why no one ever says anything because saying something means that you would become the target of abuse. The nurse shouted at me about how I shouldn't tell her how to do her job. I looked at her and asked, 'Oh, so, your job description includes discrimination and abuse?'

She continued to scream about something before storming off but I had completely zoned out. Advocating for yourself and others in the public healthcare system is important. In my experience, it is the difference between life and death, holding healthcare workers responsible for abuses of power and overall accessibility. For some bizarre reason, the public healthcare system can breed a particular type of abuse of power and lack of accountability. This is because of myriad factors: vulnerable people tend to keep their heads down, people don't feel empowered enough to demand service delivery, the fear of retaliation when we do complain, poverty and class means 'beggars can't be choosers', a lack of education and language barriers play a role because how do you complain to authorities via email if reading and writing in English is not a skill you have? How do you articulate an issue when you don't feel confident enough to do so in a language different to your mother tongue? It doesn't help that most of the senior staff and people in positions of power are white people. Even if they happened to not be racists, the power dynamics are skewed so we don't feel open to raising an issue. We have a major issue regarding human rights in South Africa. Most vulnerable people are not explicitly taught about our rights – we don't expect to be treated with basic respect and dignity. You can't really advocate for your human rights and demand that they are met if you don't know they exist. History hasn't done a very good job of showing vulnerable people that their lives matter. I used to resent my mother because I felt like she didn't care about me and refused to stand up for me even when she would admit that the treatment I received was subpar and racist. I couldn't understand how my mother could sit next to me on those old wooden benches, in a waiting room with broken windows and dirty floors, at 5 am; how she could articulate how awful it was and yet not do anything about it. I would fight back my tears, swallow the lump in my throat, and bury my face in a book wondering: 'Does she not love me? Why is she okay with putting me through this?'

My mom looked worn out, exhausted and cold – she would dress warmly, and keep the hood of her coat on, and cover herself in a big, navy-blue knitted shawl. She had to get up at 4 in the morning to get ready and get us to the hospital, where we would wait for several hours before getting me home and then go to work. She would have to work late for several evenings to make up for the half day she took off for the hospital; my mom needed to appease her bloated, perpetually red-faced tyrant of a boss.

My mom would join me during my consultations with the specialist I was transferred to after my surgery. I was pleasantly surprised that the new specialist allowed my mom to join us. Another annoying public hospital thing I hated was that you had to go in by yourself, unlike in private care where you can take someone along for emotional support. I don't really understand why they insist on it other than my conspiracy theory that it is just to dehumanise and terrorise us in private with no witnesses. The new specialist was a very skinny Indian woman, with mid-length bouncy straight dark brown hair. She seemed to perpetually hold onto a takeaway coffee cup with both of her skinny hands, her knuckles looking as if they would poke through her skin at any moment. She wore a white coat over a warm dress, with stockings and brown knee-length boots. She took small sips of coffee periodically and I wondered to myself why she sipped the coffee as if it were still hot?

She called my name and showed us to the room. She introduced herself and we exchanged pleasantries before she asked me to undress and wear a hospital gown. While I undressed, she read through my thick, manila folder, probing my mom in between for more information. I walked back into the room and she asked me to sit on the bed, my mom helped me because they didn't have a step stool and the bed's levers were broken. I sat down and my chest pounded. I was exceptionally anxious. I hadn't had any good experiences with doctors thus far and, while I was glad it was a woman, I was nervous about her being Indian. I think for most Black South Africans, we haven't experienced a lot of goodness from non-Black people, even those who are people of colour. I looked over to my mom, who was sitting on a chair in the corner of the room, holding my belongings. She looked nervous too. She gave me a small smile to assure me she was present and that I was okay. The doctor continued to look at my folder, her phone whistling repeatedly while she made notes. She came over to the bed, where I was sitting on the side, with my legs dangling down. She did a few examinations, while making notes intermittently, and then walked over to the other side of the bed and checked my neck. She put both her hands around my neck with her thin fingers gripping it firmly, she asked me to swallow as she examined my neck. I wondered what she was doing because I didn't have issues with my neck or throat at all. She brought over a metal kidney dish with vials, alcohol wipes, cotton wool and medical tape and asked me to hold still and make a fist so she could take a few blood samples for testing. I held my arm out towards her and looked away until she was done. She asked me to lie down on my back, with my legs up, pulling my knees towards my chest, and then to separate my legs so she could examine me vaginally. I felt a wave of nausea as I opened my legs. I looked up at the fluorescent lights and tried to steady my breathing. I was scared because I knew how much vaginal examinations hurt – given my own experience with them. The doctor put on white gloves and squirted lubricant on two of her fingers which she jammed into my vagina without warning. I whimpered in pain and discomfort, clenching my pelvic muscles due to the searing, burning, sharp pain. Each rotation of her fingers, each time she moved her fingers in different directions, at varying depths, felt like someone had inserted a boiling hot serrated knife inside of me. She continued her examination and then removed her fingers. I breathed in relief that it was over, before she jammed a finger into my anus, also without warning. She rotated her finger around as she had in my vagina. I wondered why she needed to examine my anus. It felt like the examination went on for a lifetime. She then removed her gloves, and started to put on a new pair when she asked me to put my legs down so she could examine my abdomen. I did as I was told. She then kneaded my belly as if she were making bread, pressing down firmly, noting where I seemed the most reactive to the pain. She told me I could get up while she made more notes, my lower back and abdomen reacting severely to the exam. It felt as if someone had kicked me. My mom helped me get up and then the doctor asked me to stand against a wall with a scale so she could note my height and weight. After this she told me I could get dressed. As I went into the small cubicle to get dressed, I could hear her ask my mom about my mood. She asked, 'Does she experience bad moods or being irritable?'

My mom answered saying, 'I guess so, like anyone else would if they felt unwell every day.'

I wondered why my mood was being discussed when I was not there to be treated for it and she didn't seem to be asking solely to establish a medical history. She retorted, 'That is unacceptable. You shouldn't allow that. Endometriosis can't be used as an excuse for being out of control.'

I opened the door and walked in before my mom could respond. She had spent all of 30 minutes with me, hardly even communicating with me, and already she thought she knew enough about me to comment on who I am, my behaviour and character. I wondered what part of dealing with an academically strong, well-adjusted young African woman, who was nervous and couldn't afford private healthcare, came from an underprivileged family on the Cape Flats made her think I was 'out of control'. My parents have never had to deal with any kind of issues that I had caused, I have never gotten into trouble, or performed poorly at school. I didn't even do the usual things teenagers and young adults did.

I sat down, unsure of what else we needed to do before I could get out of her face. She explained that she was booking an ultrasound for my next visit. She gave me a prescription for contraceptives to help with the endometriosis and pain killers. She looked at me intensively and then said to me, 'You need to lose weight, eat less and exercise a lot. You are very short and overweight and that's what is making you sick and causing all the pain and discomfort. You are over your BMI.' I looked at her, stunned. Had she not read my file? Did she not know I have endometriosis? How could my weight be responsible for my symptoms? I must have looked as if someone had just punched the air out of my lungs because I couldn't believe that she said what she said – that by looking at me, she decided that my behaviour was out of control, that I was overweight and causing my own illness and that I didn't exercise or eat healthy foods. In that moment, I felt so disempowered; I couldn't advocate for myself and defend myself. Healthcare has always been racist towards Black people, particularly women, so I wasn't exactly surprised but it still hurts. I was hardly overweight at the time but, in her world my African body looked unhealthy and overweight. I only weighed 53kg. She handed me my folder as we exited her room; I walked out in a daze. My mom asked if I was okay, I said yes and she said,

'I'm so sorry that doctor was so rude. Just keep quiet and don't rock the boat.' I hated that sentiment; I hated that I had to accept what was being said as to not 'rock the boat'. I couldn't understand my mother then. Now I get it, I understand the situation my mom was in, I understand how helpless she must have felt. She had no choice but to keep her head down too, no matter how she felt about what the doctors did or said to me or about me because she was scared they wouldn't treat me, would delay treatment or mistreat me even more. She knew how difficult it was to get specialised care and couldn't risk it because she knew she couldn't afford to go elsewhere. My mom did what she could, but her options were extremely limited.

I found out years later why the doctor checked my neck; she was trying to check if I had an issue with my thyroid that could explain why I was, in her opinion, overweight. My blood tests and further examination proved that I didn't have a thyroid issue at all. Each appointment with the doctor felt like torture. Somehow, she dismissed all my symptoms and put it down to weight. She would ask how I was coping and would visibly sigh and look annoyed when I honestly reported back on my symptoms. She gave me a referral to a psychologist and psychiatrist because she felt that my issues may be psychological because I didn't feel better. She wrote referral letters outlining how she thought I was unwell mentally and requested that the psychologist and psychiatrist consulted with me and then asked that they send her a detailed report on their findings. I gathered that she thought I was exaggerating and looking for attention from what she had said in the bits of the letter before she sealed it in an envelope. I visited the psychologist and psychiatrist, both of whom thought she was insensitive, out of line, and had no authority attempting to dissect her patients' mental states. My psychiatrist, who was quite annoyed by the situation, scoffed and said, 'What kind of patient, who is this young, dealing with stage 4 endometriosis and chronic pain, wouldn't be irritable or even depressed and anxious?'

The psychiatrist and psychologist refused to give her feedback because they didn't see why she needed it. The psychologist remarked that she couldn't understand how a doctor could assume someone's a hypochondriac when they have stage 4 endometriosis. She said, 'It's a chronic illness. Of course, you won't suddenly report no symptoms ever again.'

I still had to see the gynaecologist for my visits, with the skills my therapist taught me, so I could keep myself safe in a situation I didn't want to be in but needed to endure for the sake of my health.

I started to experience strange leg pain. It would come and go, but only happened in my left leg. It felt like sharp shooting pains and occasionally numbness when walking. It felt heavy, as if I had to drag my leg when walking, and it seemed to coincide with the endometriosis flare ups. I realised that it may be because of the endometriosis and on my next visit I told the doctor about the leg pain and numbness. She looked at me sceptically and folded her arms as I spoke. She checked my reflexes and said it was normal so there's no issue, and she told me, 'Endometriosis doesn't cause issues with the leg. It doesn't affect your legs at all, it isn't in that region.'

I said, 'But it seems to get worse when the other pain gets worse due to the endometriosis.'

She sighed and repeated what she had said in a passive aggressive tone. 'If this persists, I'll send you to a bone specialist. We deal with endometriosis and that is not endometriosis.'

There was no attempting to reason with her or getting her to understand what I was experiencing so I let it go. I knew something was horribly wrong but what else could I do? She let me know that she had put my name on the waiting list for surgery because she had tried all non-surgical options and they weren't working. I was relieved and couldn't hide it. As awful as surgery is, I would have given a kidney if it meant I didn't have to see her again. She explained to me that it could take several months before the surgeons get to me because they require multiple surgeons because of the extent of my endometriosis and the parts of my body that it had affected. At that point, I had endometriosis throughout my reproductive system, bowels and vagina. She also recommended to the surgeons that while I am under anaesthesia that they insert an IUD to assist with my painful and heavy menstrual cycles.

I waited several months until I was given a surgery date for the following July. You would have sworn my body knew I was scheduled for a surgery because suddenly the endometriosis symptoms hit me like a train. The pain was so severe that it made me feel dizzy and blinded, the digestive issues were unlike ever before – I found myself so constipated that even oral laxatives didn't help aside from causing cramping. My menstrual cycles were prolonged and painful – I would pass blood clots the size of my fist. I remember sitting on the cold wooden toilet seat in my childhood home, sweat pouring onto my chest from my face, and breathing heavily. I kept thinking, 'calm down, breathe, you have to get up so you don't scare anyone.' I didn't want to have to wake my parents up at 2 am on a wintery day, with the wind howling in my ears from the partially opened window behind me. I held onto the white porcelain basin, the contrast between the basin and the dark, thick, maroon blood pouring from my body was striking. I held on with my left hand so I could rest my head on my arm and wait for the waves of nausea and pain to release me. As I felt my mouth fill up with saliva, I tried to tell myself, 'Don't throw up, don't throw up, don't throw up', hoping that would keep me from vomiting because I hated the feeling of throwing up. The feeling of my mouth filling with saliva, my stomach constricting, the strain of heaving and muscle pain from reluctantly throwing up, before finally the brackish taste of bile in the back of my throat and then the awful feeling of the actual throwing up which seems to last for forever. I hate how I always get a cold sweat while throwing up, but I especially hated the taste and feeling after throwing up, the feeling of lingering nausea and bitterness. Before I knew it, I was throwing up into the basin, while still unable to get up from the toilet, I tried to open the tap so that my parents wouldn't hear. I looked at the contents of my stomach in the basin, a thick, greenish brown sludge, and wondered how it looked like that when I hadn't eaten anything brown or green. My mother must have heard my struggling because as I tried to clean the basin while seated on the toilet, with the most intense cramps, she knocked quietly and opened the door slightly. My mom stood there in her fleecy maroon gown and bedroom slippers, her eyes sleepy.

She asked me, 'Are you okay?' her eyes searching the view, trying to get answers.

Her eyes instantly widened as she looked at me. She looked shocked, she looked around seeing blood on the bathroom mat and on my pyjamas and the thick vomit struggling to drain in the basin. I must have looked as if I were near death. She didn't say anything – I am sure she was just too afraid to verbalise what she was thinking. She walked in and started to run some water into the bath, and threw my clothes and the mat into it. She left for a minute and came back with a change of clothes and a sanitary pad and helped me change. She started to add bleach to the basin and wiped my face with a damp cloth. She gave me some mouth wash before helping me up and putting me to bed. I felt relieved lying in my bed, the tension and cramping in my back starting to lessen. My mom came back into my bedroom with a cup of tea and some pain medication.

She sat down on my bed and asked me again, 'Are you okay? Do you need anything else?'

Her face showed her worry even though she tried to sound normal. I nodded my head and said I was okay, I just wanted to sleep. She got up and turned off the light.

She whispered in the dark room, 'I really hope this surgery makes a difference.'

How to birth your IUD and an endometrioma

AT THE TENDER AGE OF 19, I learned an invaluable lesson: my body is not mine; my body belongs to hypothetical men. Of course, although I know this to be complete and utter kak, it's still a striking 'lesson'. At the time I had been transferred to a fertility clinic under Groote Schuur. The doctors there acknowledged the severity of my endometriosis and spoke to me about my options. A tall, friendly woman with short blonde hair was assigned to me.

'Well, as you know, this is incurable – it is a life-long disease – but we have a few options we can try. We can try to induce menopause to stop your menstrual cycle, which can help control the pain. We can also try surgery again if it doesn't work and we've exhausted all our options.'

I nodded and asked, 'So, with limited options, what is the best option?'

The doctor bit down on her lip, obviously thinking very deeply about the question posed. 'People often try pregnancy as it can assist with alleviating some of the symptoms you're dealing with. I do have a colleague who could assist us and explain the background to us so we have an understanding of how it works.'

She asked if she could go get him, and I said yes.

The blonde-haired doctor returned with an older man, with salt and pepper hair and laugh lines. 'Hi, I am Doctor Matthews. I am a fertility and reproductive health specialist. Your doctor asked me to speak to you about how pregnancy assists with endometriosis symptoms.' I nodded and he continued. 'The pregnancy stops your period for several months, which can be helpful in alleviating endometriosis symptoms and pain. Another benefit is that it allows you to try to have a child now – the longer you wait the slimmer the changes of falling pregnant are.'

I sat there in a discoloured orange chair in the doctor's office, staring at a bunch of paperwork on the desk in front of me completely bewildered and afraid to make eye contact. Everything seemed to blur. 'A child? Now? Me? How?' I thought to myself. The doctor seemed to read my mind. 'We can do the fertilisation here if you would like that.'

I stuttered, 'I would rather have a hysterectomy done to help with the symptoms than a baby, I am not ready to be a parent. I don't even know if I want a child at this point in my life.' I hated feeling out of control, as if I had no say in the matter and like I was an experiment, a guinea pig, just another Henrietta Lacks? The suggestions felt more like a scare tactic.

'No, no, no,' said Doctor Matthews. 'We can't do a hysterectomy; you are too young for that. You are too young to make a decision like that.'

I felt myself tearing up, too young to choose a hysterectomy but not too young to choose a high-risk pregnancy and to raise a whole human. How sway? The blonde-haired endometriosis specialist piped up. 'And besides, what are you going to do when you meet someone and get married? What if your husband wants children? It is unfair to take that right from your husband.' Girl… I sat there feeling like Bert and Ernie from *Sesame Street*, aghast, shocked and bewildered. Are we even on the same timeline? My specialists were more concerned about some random man's 'rights', wants and needs in some future they've dreamed up, instead of my rights, needs and wants in that very moment. Who said I wanted a marriage, a husband or any of the heteronormative nonsense they were worried about? Besides, why would I want to be married to someone who cares about my keeping my womb in my body, despite the gruelling pain and discomfort? I am not the bekezela type nor am I a mbokodo type of a woman. I can't imagine bringing a child into a world where their primary function would be to keep me pain free for a few months, being born to someone who was uncertain and agreed under duress; the child born as a tick box exercise 'just in case' my condition worsens later on. It all sounded selfish and cruel to everyone involved.

The strange way men are centred added a layer of understanding and outrage that already brewed below the surface of my consciousness. In all aspects of my life, men are entitled to control, maintain and retain parts of me. That includes my fertility and ability to fulfil their dreams of being fathers, successful implantations and downright coercion in some respects. It blew my mind that a man walked into the room, who was not my doctor, and he knew absolutely nothing about me, yet he felt entitled, even emboldened, to tell me what I should do in terms of my reproductive health and future, even advocating for some man who doesn't exist and may never exist. I realised in that moment how audacious men are and how patriarchy exists in all avenues of our lives. In many ways, we view medical misconduct as an issue of the past, an apartheid issue where our grannies and moms were forcibly sterilised or injected with contraceptives against their will or even without them knowing. The truth is that generally men still have power in professions like medicine to decide the fate of the person with a womb. It is a form of control that could be dire – in my case, a pregnancy could be deadly. Pushing women to fall pregnant or keep pregnancies are actions directly responsible for children living through poverty and violence, and for unprepared parents who cannot take care of their children. It is a recipe for disaster. It is often difficult to speak to or say no to a man. In situations where the power dynamics are skewed it is even more difficult; it may be unintentional and a consequence of socialisation as a man but many men speak with authority. Even when making a suggestion, it can be hard for women to say no because of patriarchal systems. How do you say no to a doctor in a public institution without being fearful of payback?

The morning I was scheduled to report to the reception area at Groote Schuur Hospital, I recall feeling stressed and overwhelmed. I didn't know what to expect under the circumstance of an elective surgery. I had packed a bag for hospital the night before with my mom to ensure I didn't forget any basics – especially since the hospital was at least 30 minutes away by car. It was the middle of winter and my mom insisted on gowns, fluffy socks and polo fleece pyjamas even though I would be in a hospital gown. I woke up early, anticipating the day ahead. Mom and Dad were awake and rustling like leaves around the house. My dad, as usual, was impatient and tried to get us out of the house quickly to make it on time. Dad doesn't handle stressful situations well at all, he becomes anxious and argumentative. It reminds me of my 16th birthday party, an '80s-themed event with my school friends, when my dad – while hanging decorations – panicked and argued with us on a ladder about being pushed for time. He turned around, while holding decorations in place, to scold us before we heard him grunting. In turning around, he must have twisted his shoulder, which resulted in him hurting it. This was something that had happened before with my dad's shoulder, and it was my responsibility to help him pop the arm back into place. This was my due diligence for being late.

We rushed out into the chilly winter morning and got into the car all set for hospital. I was nervous and anxious – and Dad's impatience on the road wasn't helping. Halfway to the hospital, I realised that I had forgotten the necessary paperwork to submit so that they could admit me. My dad whined and scolded me about being more prepared, and blamed my mom for not ensuring the paperwork was with us. My mom shot him a look of annoyance as we returned home to grab the paperwork and get back on our way. We arrived on time and I sat down on the blue, firm plastic seats waiting for the admin office to open up. The lights in the admin section were turned on but only one clerk seemed to be present. He raised the old off-white blinds from his cubicle window and motioned for us to come through. The entire process was swift and he quickly checked the paperwork and printed stickers with all my information on them. He stapled the infamous paperwork and newly printed stickers to my hospital folder and told us to go to the gynaecological ward. My parents accompanied me to the ward and we were asked to wait for some time because the nurses were in the middle of swapping shifts and doing handovers of the patients they were observing. We waited at the nurses' station until a nurse came to look at my folder and check that all the paperwork was in order before ushering me to my bed. She told my parents that they wouldn't be able to stay but they could help me settle in. My mom immediately started making my bed and added a warm fluffy pink blanket and took out my gown from the bag to drape it over the bottom of the bed in case I needed it. She placed my books on the bedside table next to me and checked that I had my phone and charger. We said our goodbyes quickly and they assured me they would come by for the evening visit. I settled into bed, and the nurse pulled up a chair and the tray table to place my folder on and asked me an array of standard questions before surgery. The nurse asked her questions in a bored and disinterested tone; I could tell it was simply protocol. She asked me if I had any medical conditions, while looking up at me over the rim of her glasses. I was flustered and suddenly couldn't remember, 'Uh … no, I don't think so. Wait, yes … I have asthma? Does that count?' I asked her nervously. She said it did.

'Do you smoke? Do you do drugs? Do you drink alcohol? I have to ask for the sake of a medical history.'

I looked at her sheepishly and answered, 'No, no. I don't do any of those.'

She looked at me and smiled, 'Okay, my darling. Do you think there is a chance you could be pregnant?' I was shocked at the question; I remember wondering why she would ask me that. Obviously, in retrospect, I realise it is a necessary question.

'No, there is no chance I could be pregnant.'

Once she had finished all of the necessary questions, she wrote my name on my hospital armband along with my identification number and which ward I was in. The nurse let me know that I was scheduled for surgery first thing the following morning and that I would need to stay the night for them to monitor my vitals and for them to prepare me for surgery. This included an enema to clear my bowels in case I needed surgery there. I listened and nodded as she spoke. I had already figured they may want me to stay for monitoring beforehand. She showed me the legal paperwork wherein it stated the type of surgery they would be performing, including potential risks and possible interventions. She read it to me slowly, pausing and looking at me after each new paragraph to ensure I understood each part of what she was saying.

'The hospital is not responsible for any lost or stolen items which you may have brought along with you.' I nodded in agreement. 'There is a risk of bleeding, infection, or even death with any surgery.' She looked up at me and I felt anxious but let her know I understood. 'In the event of bleeding, you are consenting to a blood transfusion and any other means to resuscitate?' The idea of someone else's blood coursing through my veins made me naar but I understood the need. I swallowed and nodded yes. She also told me I would have to sign and agree to the surgery and that I understand the risks involved, as well as agreeing to the fact that the surgeons were preparing to insert a Mirena while I was in theatre. I signed the paperwork and handed it back to the nurse and settled back into bed, anxious about the surgery and how I would keep my mind occupied for the day while waiting.

I couldn't figure out whether the ward seemed gloomy or if it was because of my head space but everything seemed more muted than usual. The sunlight streaming in seemed less bright, the curtains were a candied striped design but the colours all seemed like shades of grey, even the people in the ward with me looked like they were pale or like a grey filter had been applied on them all. I tried to nap so time could pass by faster but the ward was fairly loud and my bed was right next to the nurses' station. In between multiple calls, alarms, loud talking and patients calling for nurses it was a difficult task to fall asleep. The woman opposite me seemed especially loud and bizarre. She was a skinny older woman with short natural hair. She seemed restless, spoke to herself and got up out of bed frequently. She randomly called for the nurses every 10 minutes or so for seemingly no reason. She seemed to agitate everyone in the room who was ill, post-surgery or just down because of being hospitalised. The woman directly next to me must have noticed my discomfort because she turned to me and smiled at me and told me her name. She said the woman was harmless, and nothing to worry about. She just didn't sit for very long and liked to talk. I smiled back at her and nodded. The evening passed by fast, and my parents and sister arrived at the hospital with supper. With me sitting up in my hospital bed, my sister and my childhood best friend sitting on my bed, my parents, aunt, uncle, my friend's father all stood around my bed talking and laughing about everything under the sun, including how peaceful I seemed for someone going into surgery. They had brought my favourite snacks and food so I could stuff myself before I was no longer allowed to eat. They stayed the hour and, before they headed out, they wished me well for my surgery in the morning.

The nurse came by after visiting hours and laughed at my bedside table covered in food and snacks. 'You know you have to stop eating by 10 pm, ne? You must also still do your enema to clear your bowels before surgery.

I smiled at her, and said, 'I know, I won't forget! That's why I ate everything I could now.' We both laughed as she walked off.

Morning came fast. I was awoken by the nurse before other

patients because I was first on the theatre list. She noticed I was anxious and tried to keep me calm. She let me know I would be allowed to take anti-anxiety medication if I wanted to and I agreed. She came back and shut the hospital curtains surrounding my bed before giving me the anxiety medication and instructing me to lie on my side, facing away from her so that she could administer the enema. As she finished, she told me to lay down in the position for at least 20 minutes before going to the bathroom. After my enema and subsequent bathroom trip, I was instructed to shower and pack my belongings away securely as I was about to be taken to the theatre for surgery.

I nervously waited for my mom to arrive so I could give her my phone and say goodbye to her before being taken to theatre. My mom arrived just in time before the porters came to escort me to theatre. They arrived with a gurney, and I was asked to get onto it. My mom gave me one last hug and assured me that everything would be fine, and that she would see me when I woke up.

The trip from the ward to the theatre section felt like a lifetime, everything felt slowed down and I felt anxious the nearer we got. We arrived at a massive door and the porters told me that the team would be with me shortly. The surgeon wasted no time and almost immediately came out and asked me a few questions as he wheeled me through the massive doors into a smaller room with shelves on either side of me, holding stacks of towels. The surgeon introduced himself and let me know the team was ready and went over the consent forms with me.

Soon, two younger doctors in scrubs came in and then a middle-aged nurse rubbed my arm and let me know she would be present. The team then wheeled me into the operating room which shocked me because during my previous surgery, I had been sedated in a room just outside the actual operating room and not in it. The room looked like they do in the movies. The lights were bright and blinding; there seemed to be equipment and machinery everywhere and people unidentifiable under their protective wear. They told me they would be sliding me onto a smaller, uncomfortable looking bed which would be used during my surgery. The room was freezing – I was visibly shaking and attempting to cover myself as much as I could with the single blanket. The surgeon said unfortunately they had to keep the operating room cold and that I would soon be under. As they transferred me to the other bed, the anaesthesiologist introduced herself and told me she would be monitoring me through my surgery. She asked me for my arm so that she could insert an IV. I looked away as she inserted it, and then she put a secured mask on my face and asked me to count back from 10. I started strongly, 10, 9, 8… before fading off into a slumber.

When I woke up, I was back in the busy ward I had left that morning, in the same bed, as if no time had passed at all. I felt groggy, disorientated and annoyed by the business within the ward. Students pacing around with doctors to examine patients, loud talking, busy nurses, patients loudly discussing their discomfort. The sun seemed to be glaring over the top of Table Mountain directly into my eyes; my eyelids were heavy but the sun distracted me. I fell in and out of consciousness, my abdomen ached and I wondered where my mom was. I thought she would be there when I woke up but she wasn't and I panicked wondering where my mom was in the state of grogginess. I had no way of calling her because she had taken my phone along with her.

I asked a nurse who passed by where my mom was and she said, 'Don't worry, mommy will come soon.'

I felt out of sorts and panicked and the kind older woman next to me noticed and came to my bedside with her phone. She said she didn't have a smartphone but if I knew my mom's number she could call her. I gave her my mom's number and she called her. I must have slipped into a slumber because the kind woman woke me gently and told me she had spoken to my mom and that my mom was on her way. When I woke up several hours later, my mom was indeed there and had been for a few hours. She had brought me some soup and juice, and my phone. I felt a lot less anxious and out of sorts; I felt like myself although in pain. The pain wasn't nearly as severe as the pain I felt during the first surgery.

Later that evening, my sister, brother, parents, aunt and uncle, two friends and their parents visited me. They rallied around my bed, and I was well enough to sit up and talk to them. They tried to cheer me up and brought me snacks and covered me in love. They all seemed surprised at my ability to be sitting up and holding a conversation. My friend asked me, 'How on earth are you sitting up, bru, you just had surgery…'

I laughed and said, 'Well, this surgery wasn't nearly as bad as the first one, and you mos know my pain threshold is Mount Everest.'

My family laughed at my nonsense, while my nosy brother Matthew looked through my files, interpreting my ECG and doctors' notes. Matthew joked, 'Nadine is basically bionic after this.'

My sister playfully scolded him for reading my file.

The surgeon came by the next morning to check on me and gave me an update on the findings. In a concerned tone, he told me that the endometriosis was quite extensive. 'We found that your left fallopian tube and left ovary were stuck to your uterus; we had to detach them. We also found that your bowel had adhered to the posteriofundal aspect of your uterus. Your pouch of Douglas was partially obliterated, which could be the reason for your coccyx pain. We also found the presence of endometriosis on both uterosacral ligaments, which could also account for the pain you experience in your left leg.'

I looked at him, trying to keep up with what this meant even though it was being simplified but, truthfully, I just wanted to know when I could go home and rest. I asked when I would be able to go home and he said, considering I had asked for my catheter to be removed, was stable and able to mobilise, I would be able to go home the very next day. I sighed out of relief as I would much rather recover at home.

The following day, the doctor and nurses came around to do

their checks, fill out paperwork and go over what had been done. They reiterated the fact that they had inserted a Mirena so I would not need to use oral contraceptives, and that they would be sending me home with pain medication and a note for a check-up. They left to get my discharge papers finalised and I was elated. I thought I had a new lease on life and that my life would be a little bit less complicated going forward.

My recovery period was uneventful and I returned to life as usual. I returned to university determined to just live my life as best as I could even though it would never be just the same as my peers. Due to the Mirena, I had at least one less thing to worry about, which was a debilitating monthly period. I still had endometriosis symptoms but they were less severe, especially without the monthly bleeding.

Early the following year, I was at a restaurant with my sister and felt really strange – I had a throbbing lower back ache and what felt like period pain, although I did not have my period. I went to the restroom at the restaurant and checked but I was not bleeding at all. I decided to go back and join the rest of the dinner. I figured it was just an endometriosis flare up and that the uncomfortable seating was just aggravating my symptoms. As the evening progressed, I felt nauseous and the pain seemed to come on stronger and in waves.

My sister took me home, and I got ready for bed. I jokingly said to my mom that I felt as if I were in labour. Not that I had ever been but from how people describe contractions, the pain seemed to come on faster and for longer as the evening progressed. My mom suggested I get some rest; she made me some tea and I settled down with my hot water bottle and some pain medication. I followed her orders and fell asleep, but in the early hours of the morning, I woke up in stabbing pain. I threw the duvet off my body as I sat up and noticed that I was bleeding and had been for some time since the bedding was crimson. I was in shock; confused and dizzy, I shouted for help from my mom and tried to get up and hold my legs together in an attempt to not bloody anything on my way to the bathroom. My mom shoved my bedroom door open and looked at me in shock; I was in pain and pale. My mom assisted me to the bathroom, I sat down and tried to wipe away the blood so I could examine my vagina, I couldn't figure out where I was bleeding from entirely or the reason for the stabbing and contracting pain. I wiped and realised that there seemed to be a metal string hanging from the opening of my vagina, I panicked naturally, unsure of how on earth I was going to explain to anyone how I had a metal draatjie hanging from my doos and had no idea how it got there. I had forgotten about the Mirena inserted in surgery and I had not seen it, but had read that it had a metal string that should be located higher and not come down. In my state of panic, I thought of Dr Sindi van Zyl whom I had I met via Twitter due to her concern for women's health and advocacy. I screamed for my mom to get me my phone and to pack a bag, while I sent Dr Sindi van Zyl a message. I knew she would be awake since she considered herself a card-carrying member of the Natural Short Sleeper gang. I asked her whether I should just pull it out like a tampon and move on or if I needed to seek medical attention. Dr Sindi responded swiftly and sternly to tell me not to pull on anything but to go the trauma unit at the hospital where I had my surgery done, explaining I could cause internal damage or infection. I thanked her and quickly rushed to Groote Schuur Hospital.

It seemed quiet enough but their larger trauma unit sent us to a trauma section particularly for gynaecology and obstetrics emergencies. I was taken to a small section where there were three other women: an elderly woman who disclosed she had uterine cancer, a young girl who seemed dishevelled, scared and silent and her mom, and me attempting to not screech for assistance. My mom was allowed in the section with me, and she tried to keep me distracted but the contraction-like feeling seemed more persistent. I told my mom I felt intense pressure and felt like I needed to go to the bathroom. The nurse said I couldn't because she needed to make sure I got examined first. I tried to sit through it, hoping I would be called soon, but within a few minutes I gave in and walked myself to the bathroom without the nurse's permission. My legs shook anxiously as I sat down on the dirty toilet. I was sweating profusely, still bleeding, and it felt like I was getting ripped wide open. I felt the pressure worsen and I just pushed as a way to keep the pain at bay. I heard my mom at the door frantic because I had locked it. I pushed and grunted in pain and suddenly heard a loud thump into the toilet bowl, sudden relief and the disgust of toilet bowl water splashing onto me. I sat there relieved and tried to collect myself so I could open the door and let my mom see, and also see for myself what kind of a blood clot could cause so much pain. I opened the door and a nurse and my mom immediately grabbed at me and assisted me. I was in complete shock; the toilet water had a red tint and the thing in the toilet bowl was like nothing I had ever seen. My mom looked stunned, the nurse screamed for another nurse to bring some equipment, who removed the thing from the toilet bowl and quickly put it in a specimen bag to be identified. She helped my mom sit me down before she ran in to rush the doctor along and insist I be seen next. I felt exhausted and just wanted to leave as soon as possible. I heard the nurses say, 'The Mirena was in the specimen as well!' I found it funny how suddenly everyone started to speak like we were in an episode of Dexter's Laboratory.

Soon, an unfriendly, thin, scraggly, blonde-haired doctor opened the door. She shouted 'Dirks!' abruptly while looking at my file. She made no eye contact.

I struggled up in pain with my mom's assistance before the doctor said I had to come in alone. She looked like the perfect depiction of a witch in an animation, just cold and unkind. The room was dark for some reason; she had the blinds closed and the only light on seemed to be the one for examinations. She told me to undress into a gown and lie down on the bed so that she could examine me. I did as I was told. Soon, she pulled away the curtains, sat down on a wheely chair, and pushed herself towards me with my file in her hand. She asked me invasive questions about whether I was sexually active with multiple people, whether I had a history of STIs and STDs, how many pregnancies I had had. I answered her truthfully but she seemed unfazed, as if she had already decided my fate. She kind of spoke under her breath about how people like me always act like we have no idea as to why we are presenting with particular symptoms. She seemed convinced I had pelvic inflammatory disease. She made a few notes before putting on a set of gloves, separating my legs and using the biggest speculum she could find – another doctor using this as a way to punish me for undoubtedly lying about whatever the cause of my pain and bleeding was. Even though my file clearly stated I had stage 4 endometriosis.

I winced in pain and naturally contracted my muscles, and this annoyed the doctor even more. She snapped and told me, 'You are only making this worse for yourself!'

I tried to disappear into a different world so I could escape her torment. She finished her examination and concluded nothing was wrong with me; my Mirena had come out and I needed to get up and clean myself up. She threw a few paper towels on the bed and a pad and told me to clean myself up and I did as I was told in a daze, wondering if I were simply being dramatic or if this was just what people experienced. I tried to hold back my tears, fearing that she would further shout at me, and I got dressed. I started panicking, realising I had a massive assignment to finish that was due the following evening and had no time to work on it. The pain was crushing and I tried to ask the doctor for a note to excuse me for another day so I could rest and finish my assignment. She looked at me with annoyance and disgust and scoffed at me. She said, 'For what? You just want a day off. There is nothing wrong with you.' She shut the door in my face.

The nurse who had assisted earlier seemed sympathetic and told me to take some paracetamol and to go to the trauma centre if I developed a fever or if the pain worsened. I tried to ignore the pain and proceed with the day and just keep going and believing I was completely fine and that the experience was not traumatic.

I completed my assignment while in pain and bleeding because I didn't want to be seen as dramatic and I didn't want to affect my studies. Surely, if a doctor says that I am fine, then I should be fine? I pushed the experience out of my mind and moved on, leaving it in an unopened box until a therapy session when I realised how traumatic and painful it was. I had to sit with the thought that, in any other situation, someone using a large object to shove inside of my vagina to 'punish' me would have been considered sexual assault. This was no different to that. The realisation of what had actually happened to me comes in waves and is something that I still have difficulty reconciling. The effects of power and privilege and how that impacts someone's interaction and their disregard for another woman's body is enraging and disturbing. Just like in *Animal Farm*, it is obvious that some animals truly are more equal than others.

Just a bietjie white supremacy and a dash of privilege

IT'S NOT LIKE I DIDN'T know racism and discrimination existed or anything but I guess in some ways I naively thought work may be a little bit less awful than the rest of the 'real' world or at least a bit more subtle. One of my earliest corporate roles in the pee-drenched Cape Town Central Business District, at an uphill walk from the bus terminus, proved to be hell on earth. Not only because of the stench of pee, but more so because the walk threatened to push my poor body to the edge in business casual kitten heels. I would go through the five stages of grief daily, because the role itself seemed relatively easy but the founders, a wealthy family, annoyed me to no end. The balding middle-aged son with his thin ties that looked like garden snakes and brown shoes that resembled Toughees school shoes, always drove me up the wall. He would march down rows of employees in an open plan office like a Micromanaging Dictator. For some reason, he marched with a smug face, saying, 'Looks good, awesome, ja no hey!' until he reached the target of choice: 'This is not up to standard! This is bloody shit!'

He panted and paced in hysteria, turning red from ear to ear, suddenly dripping sweat before marching off in a huff of rage. Mostly, I kept my head down, spending lunch eating at my desk and watching Buzzfeed videos. I decided to unpack my things to be stored on my desk. As a chronically ill person, I put my medication on my desk along with a cactus, hand sanitiser and hand cream.

Just as I finished, the random woman next to me, with big eyes so dark you couldn't see her pupils and long dark hair, piped up in a condescending tone, 'Those pain killers are very addictive, you shouldn't be taking them just for minor pain.'

I turned my chair to look at her directly and took a second before deciding whether I was going to slap her or ignore her. I looked at her blankly and said, 'Oh okay, thanks.' I couldn't believe this woman and her liver of an ox; I turned my chair back to my desk and put my headphones on. Imagine that? Telling someone about their own medical condition. I recall just being astounded to the point of nearly laughing to myself.

Now, don't get me wrong, I never for a second misunderstood the situation of blatant racism, white privilege and white supremacy, but it is a helluva drug. I can still picture the human resources woman, a sickly thin, dark-haired woman with big blue eyes, nearly next to my office chair and resting her thin hand on my thigh before giving me a stern talking to about arriving late to work for two consecutive days. How late? Well, a whole minute! And the next day, a whole 48 seconds late. I tried to explain how awful traffic was and that public transport was a nightmare, especially while being disabled. The poppie however looked at me bewildered and stated she lived even further and got to work on time – in her sleek new car, of course. I tried to keep from rolling my eyes and headbutting the life out of her.

Poppie said to me, 'This is your last warning, hey? Next time, it will have to be a written warning. You have to make an effort to get up earlier and get here, okay?' Her voice was supremely irritating.

Later the same day, my manager, whose face hardly moved because of all the Botox, asked me, 'Do you have any idea where Carla is? I haven't heard from her yet.'

I looked at my computer. It was 11:45 am, and Carla was missing in action. I hadn't heard from her, no one else had. My manager hopped onto the landline and tried several times before reaching Carla. She erupted into laughter, slapping her thigh and letting Carla know to 'sleep it off'. Evidently, Carla had gone to Long Street after work, drank too many cheap shots and couldn't wake up for work.

Since it was beyond 8:30 in the morning, in our workplace rulebook this meant we were to inform our direct line manager if we were not going to make it or suffer disciplinary action.

Botox Barbie hung up with Carla and beamed retelling how Carla was not coming in because she was hungover. 'Ah... to be young again,' she mused.

HR joined in and said, 'Let her enjoy it, we've all been there.'

At this point, I was certain I was getting punk'd because how could this possibly be the reaction within the same day I was publicly chastised for being less than a minute late? It had to be a joke, surely. Turns out, it is not a joke – all you have to do is be born white and suddenly the rules don't apply to you or you are entitled to more flexibility based on being 'young', which was ridiculous given that I was in fact 23, and Carla was already 27 years old. I couldn't get over the audacity, how they felt like they could say all this right in front of me, without allotting me the same freedoms. Carla continued to pull this stunt several times.

On a particularly overcast day, in the car with my sister who was giving me a lift to work, I was overcome with pain. My lower back and pelvic area felt like it was being pulled in multiple directions. My sister looked over at me and said, 'Are you okay? You look like you're about to pass out?'

I tried to adjust myself but the pain hit me in waves. By the time we got to my sister's workplace, she insisted I go see a doctor. She told me, 'Seriously ... screw this job and these people, if they don't understand you don't feel well, then honestly ... it is not a job or environment for you.'

I nodded while my sister arranged a lift for me and sent me

home. I emailed to let Botox Barbie know I would not be coming in as I was in severe pain, to which she didn't respond. I then opted to WhatsApp her, which she blue ticked. I spiralled into a fit of panic, wondering whether I should borrow money for a note from a doctor or go to the local clinic and spend the day in a crowded space, with nowhere to sit while in pain so I could prove I wasn't just a skelm. I panicked and hyperventilated until I somehow passed out. Later that day, I thought about it and decided to send a follow-up email asking if I needed a note or not. My manager said if I intended to stay home again, I would need one. I decided to go to see a doctor who decided I was not fit to be trekking across the city for a stressful job daily.

My doctor urged me to ask them if I could work from home, which, to be honest, would have been perfectly fine since everything I did could be done remotely anyway. 'I will write a motivation letter if I need to, you can't be putting your body under such immense pressure.' His face was a mixture of concern and frustration.

I told him I would ask but it was unlikely that they'd agree.

I sent an email to my manager, HR and my doctor explaining the situation and the solution my doctor had provided. No one responded for days, until my phone rang – it was HR calling me. I looked down at my phone nervously, almost paralysed with fear, wondering what she'd say. I answered the phone and before I could even attempt to exchange pleasantries, she told me in a stern tone that I was being insubordinate, and I would not be able to get special treatment. Either I come back to work the following Monday as per my sick note or lose my job. Her tone, word choice and just sheer audacity made me want to tell her exactly where to get off but I held back in an attempt to be professional. I frantically tried to reason and figure out what to do: working that job was not sustainable in the least but I also couldn't be unemployed. I had so much going through my head: What would I do? Eat? How would I afford my necessary medications? By the end of the week, I had come to the realisation that I needed to quit, as there was no way I would ever be treated like Carla, and I would not be able to stay without absolutely losing my mind. I sent in a letter of resignation with a two-week notice period as required but I was finally given a taste of the fine privilege. They decided to forgo the two-week notice period and rather get rid of me and pay me for the two weeks, severing ties immediately.

I have never been so overjoyed to lose a job. It was hellish and until today I cannot fathom how ubiquitous white supremacy is, and how people have no issue with being obvious about it. Not a subtle bone in their bodies. I hope Crackling Carla, Botox Barbie and Haggard HR are doing better at life, with some necessary lessons and people skills but, honestly... I would not hold my breathe. Some people just don't have it in them to introspect and evolve. In truth, I am just glad I never have to sit through HR's skinny paws on my thigh ever again!

Funny enough, I have had to engage in many more such instances of wild behaviour from employees. From my health compromising my work and being told by the director of an NPO that 'We took a chance on you!' to a director at an agency telling me to consider doing consultancy work instead. As if a consultancy doesn't require experience, connections and often a bietjie nepotism.

I started a job at communications agency and I was so excited to finally be in a space with a team who I deemed to be more socially aware. I knew two of the women from Twitter and they seemed to be 'woke'. The one woman became my manager and the other was a director. They were sisters and what I would consider 'Fairways Coloureds', you know ... the English-speaking ones with the straight hair.

It didn't take long for me to realise there was trouble in paradise. My manager Lauren was often absent for hours on end. She would book appointments to have her nails and hair done during working hours, and the team deeply distrusted her. For a brief moment, they even distrusted me because they could not fathom how I knew them and, if I did, I was likely a foot soldier for them. The team soon loosened up and told me, 'Yoh, we were nervous, we thought you were related to Lauren and Sandra, so we didn't want to talk much and get into trouble.' I was naturally taken aback and couldn't fully comprehend it until I witnessed Lauren blaming people within the team for her errors and absence. Lauren also had no educational background in media, marketing, communications or the like, and her sister got her the job as a manager. Sandra, on the other hand, would support Lauren in blaming a team of young Black and brown people.

The reaction to my living in Mitchell's Plain was hilarious, you'd have sworn I had just said I was going to stab someone. As the saying goes… 'it really do be your own.' My face must have changed to a look of 'Are you jas?' because Lauren quickly changed her tone and said, 'Oh, I mean because shame, you travel far!' Why, yes, yes, I do, so now can we consider that reasonable accommodation?

It was jarring, from the people on Twitter who went off day and night about how anti-Blackness was common in the Black community and how messed up white supremacy was. Lauren and Sandra very clearly tried their hardest to get close to me as the new person, I'm sure, as a way to better control and blame the team when they needed to. I tried to play nice and go to the lunches and coffee dates that excluded my colleagues, with an awareness that they were backhanded. On one such coffee trip Sandra whipped out a small glass bottle she had filled with some of her hair serum to give me. 'Here, use this on your fly-aways, so your hair won't look so dry.' I took the bottle from her, completely bewildered at the gesture, wondering whether she was being kind and maternal or rude.

My endometriosis didn't take long before it started to kick my butt just because of the physical strain of working fulltime, taking public transport and having to walk uphill daily. I found myself using a hot water bottle at work and needing to wear comfortable shoes, limiting my walking and taking time off when things got too bad.

I expressed my anxiety and panic that the constant up and downs would impact my job to Sandra. By this point, both Sandra and Lauren had given up trying to be my friend – they had both realised it was a fruitless exercise, so I quickly became part of the teamwide bullying and blaming for their mistakes. Sandra looked at me and snidely said, 'Well, if it's an issue for you, then you should go and start a consultancy. That way you can work for yourself and how you want.'

Her comment and tone enraged me. It was just so out of touch, unsupportive and ridiculous. In what world is it a possibility to just quit your job with a few months' worth of experience and start a consultancy? I suppose for people who gave jobs to family members it seemed like a completely rational thing to say. I would have expected in their social justice online warrior mode they would consider reasonable accommodations like working from home when I had difficult days but that would be too much to ask.

I left soon after the manager made another colossal mistake and the entire team ended up in a hearing getting shouted at. I distinctly remember being asked in the hearing that I should consider whether my activist brand was more important to me than the company values.

To that I asked: What values? I tendered my resignation the next day.

My so-called activist brand had started years ago when I was 14 when my mom's best friend died from complications due to HIV/AIDS. I felt so helpless and lost, I needed to do something. I needed to raise awareness so others could understand the pain of losing a loved one because of a system that doesn't work. At the time President Thabo Mbeki and Health Minister Manto Tshabalala-Msimang were denialists causing the unnecessary deaths of many due to a lack of access to anti-retrovirals.

The privilege to be able to resign and send an angry letter, taking one for the team who all had major responsibilities while I lived at home with my parents, is not lost on me. My parents scoffed when

I told them what happened. My dad shook his head, saying, 'You were an activist long before these people met you!'

My parents let me know that the job caused me more setbacks than it provided growth, and gave me the courage and, in many ways, the unsaid permission, to quit.

The fact of it is that the intersections of our lives don't matter. If you are Black, a woman, queer, disabled or anything out of the box of 'normal', you are a freakshow worthy of being treated with disdain. And God help you if you happen to have many of these marginalised identities intersecting because then you are in for a ride. Disability as a white person is very different to the experience of a disabled person who is Black. The is no room for reasonable accommodation – somehow, we don't deserve it and it is deemed 'wanting to be treated like one is special', which is a madness! All we want is to be accommodated and treated with the same regard as others. I am sure my case is especially confusing, because people expect disabilities to have a look, something they can name and just spot immediately. They don't understand that disabilities look different and some are not visible. So, I would imagine my walking into the office daily without some kind of walking aid had to cause confusion and maybe even gossip. 'How is she disabled? She walks and looks fine to me.' This is the general departure point for many who simply don't seem to know better.

The thing about being disabled, though, is the expectation that all disabled people act, look and experience the world in a particular way. It is almost an expectation that in order to be seen as actually disabled, you have to perform a role for able-bodied people and, if you don't, you run the risk of being denied reasonable accommodations. It is a bizarre situation to be in, as if the only way to be accommodating of us is to be in control, not to give us the resources we need to be self-sufficient and rather just enough for us to be dependent and at the mercy of those who are judging our disabilities and attempting to grade our disabilities in a hierarchy of sorts. If you are disabled, you have to be the extraordinary disabled person, one who performs like an able-bodied individual or else. But how can you be taken seriously in the workplace when your disability has implications on your work if you are not provided with tools to assist you?

Regrets and losses

IF I AM BEING COMPLETELY candid, ever since I was introduced to the importance of my oven, people have continued to show me how important my oven is to them. From congratulating me on my first period to being concerned about my ability to conceive. It's been a repetitive conversation about my oven and not in a good way. Whenever someone speaks to me and tries to figure out how I feel about being chronically ill, especially with an issue that affects my reproductive health, they tend to ask me about babies and a husband. It is bizarre how people manage to project their lives and experiences onto someone else. Now, after everything I've been through, reader, do you think a marriage and children are the first things on my mind? If I were to get married, I would want to get married to someone who cared about me as a person, and not my reproductive abilities. As for a baby? Surely, we have enough babies on this earth who need parents?

No one ever asks me, 'But what do you regret? What have you found challenging with a chronic illness? The answer is simple: My ability to do things. My symptoms started so early in my life that, honestly, I don't remember what it's like to play, to do things my peers were doing. I don't recall being able to run around in the hot sun with the loose sand of the Cape Flats beneath my bare feet. I didn't get to play tok-tokkie on the neighbour's doors before bolting to hide behind an aunty's malva bushes, I couldn't play drie blikkies or seetle-seet with my friends and cousins because I couldn't keep up. Those are the things I missed out on; those are the losses that I most regret because it stole my childhood. I never got to try out for school athletics with my friends or do the physical aspects of PE classes with my classmates. I have had to cancel on fun activities with my friends because I had my period and just felt blinded by the level of pain I was in. I would contemplate whether I should force myself and join my friends but I knew I couldn't participate. It is a catch-22 situation: either I go and try to enjoy myself through the pain or I stay home and feel down and like I was missing out.

Endometriosis has made me a bystander. I don't remember what it is like to live without back pain because it was one of my first symptoms. This feeling of being a bystander in my own life hasn't gone away at all, it is a feeling that has lingered below the surface since I was a child. In high school when all my peers were attending parties, going to the beach together, playing sports and sneaking into clubs and bars, I was at home, with my hot water bottle, tea, pain killers and a book. I missed out on so many milestones and experiences that form part of the overall experience of being a young person exploring and adventuring. When my friends arranged hiking trips, instead of being honest about my abilities, my instinct was to just pretend that I didn't like to hike and that it sounded boring. In reality, I would sit at home watching their social media updates and long to be hiking and having fun with them.

Endometriosis cut my matric ball short because I was in too much pain to stay and keep dancing with my friends. Instead, I had to go home, take a hot bath, prepare a hot water bottle and take pain medication while watching my friends' social media updates. My first year of high school, I joined the Junior Rangers and trained with nature conservationists at the South African National Parks. I was elated to be chosen to join the programme and hang out with other teens who were interested in the environment. I counted down the days to the next meeting because it was always a good time throwing caution to the wind. Junior Rangers was a comedy show of education. I recall one particularly frightening, yet funny, occurrence. We were about a kilometre away from our classroom listening to the teacher drone on and on about mussels, perlemoen and the Rocky Shores when we heard a loud crash. We all looked over in shock to find the teacher's white Camry implanted into the wall from the impact of the crash. The group started to walk back towards the classroom wondering whether the car had rolled somehow, only to discover that a troop of baboons had decided to go into the classroom and steal all our food and the car keys and load it all in the car. They must have somehow released the handbrake in the process of cramming into the car, before running off with the food.

Soon I became a bystander even within my niche friend group – I just couldn't keep up and hop on rocks at the beach, go hiking up Slang Kop to look for blooming ericas, or walk for hours on end. I ended up leaving the programme after I was scolded for missing several classes. Each time it was because of my period and I was in horrible pain and bleeding heavily. I was heart-sore to have another aspect of my life swiftly come to an end.

Living with endometriosis means that I have mastered seeming like I am doing fine when I am struggling and in severe pain. I would not mention it, because I didn't want anyone feeling bad for me, and I didn't want to burden others and spoil their fun. This disease has robbed me of celebrating many important milestones and enjoying many experiences. It has made every day a challenge – a challenge to keep up, to keep a brave face, to power through the pain. These losses have made me a stranger to my peers because they can't relate to me, as we don't enjoy the same things or frequent the same places. How do you relate to a 21-year-old who is in too much pain to get up, and spends her evenings in bed, with a book and a heating pad? By the time I was done for the day and my body was complaining about the smallest amount of activity, my peers were only just getting ready for the club. I don't even know if I like clubs. I find them loud, crowded, stuffy and hot but having the choice made for me as to whether I can go or not is what bothers me most.

Endometriosis has shattered so many dreams of mine. At one point in high school I was passionate about food and wanted to go to culinary school or to study medicine and become a doctor. I was so set on my career options and even got brochures for courses to share with my parents, who always seemed to get unusually quiet when I mentioned what I wanted to pursue. Eventually they had to be honest with me because I was in denial about my abilities. My mom looked at me with sadness and said, 'Nadine ... you can't be a chef or a doctor, it's not realistic... How will you manage jobs that require you to be on your feet, running up and down for hours on end? It won't work.'

I looked at her with anger because I felt like she was crushing my dreams. I looked over to my dad, hoping he would intervene and talk some sense into my mother who had clearly lost it.

My dad looked at me, and was silent for a few seconds before saying, 'I agree, you can't do a hospital in-service or the pressures of being on your feet in a hot kitchen for hours, it will just cause your symptoms to flare.'

I stormed off to my bedroom in anger before the hot tears started streaming down my face. 'How could they be so mean and unsupportive?' I asked myself. I was gutted and had no plan B. What was I going to do if I couldn't be a chef or a doctor? Why couldn't I just do it and then decide if it is for me? I now realise that for my working-class parents, who had managed to leave their lives in a shack in gang-infested Hanover Park as a means to provide better for their children, allowing me to see for myself just wasn't a financial option. I know it shattered them knowing they could not provide more opportunities and even made them feel like they had failed me because they just didn't have the financial freedom to allow me to explore.

By the time I started university, I had just been diagnosed and operated on a few months prior. I remember bleeding every single day during my first year of university to the point of getting a diaper rash from the constant use of night pads. The feeling of being a bystander and not truly experiencing university and my early twenties continued. I would listen to my friends and classmates talk about their university experience and freedoms and it was so different to mine. Most were attending lectures, getting ready for the club and somehow fresh as a daisy the next morning for lectures. I marvelled at them because I felt like I was hungover most days. They would whip out their phones and show videos and photos of themselves in Long Street, drinking R1 shots, laughing and dancing the night away before inevitably recording someone throwing up outside a sketchy bar. They had the most interesting stories about the people they had met, someone who seemed interested in one of the girls, how they managed to drink for free. It always sounded like they had the most incredible time eating their youth, as the kids say. I would just be the friend who got to look at the photos and videos. In a sense I was vicariously living through them, and experiencing clubs, bars and dancing all night with them through glimpses via photos and short clips. They had inside jokes from their partying that I wasn't privy to and I had become so accustomed to watching from the side lines that it didn't bother me all that much.

Living with endometriosis has made me unrelatable to my peers, understandably so. How many twenty-something-year-olds, who 'look' healthy but are unable to climb multiple flights of stairs do you know? There aren't many 19-year-olds who are battling the heat because they're going through medically induced menopause. I have had to carve out paths for myself in unchartered territory. I couldn't follow the straightforward ideals and societal expectations of what milestones are meant to look like. I couldn't experience the phases people talk about, I mean... how could I possibly have a clubbing phase? I have had to really soul search and figure out what it is I enjoy, what I can do that my body allows, and I have learned to be patient and kind to myself and my body.

One of the most difficult aspects of endometriosis at this stage and severity means that I am watching myself deteriorate, slowly realising I am unable to do simple things I could do even a year ago, like painting my own toenails. I find myself watching people dance and feeling a sense of sadness and defeat because I love to dance. Dancing was something my sister and I did growing up: we'd turn my sister's bedroom into a club by turning off the lights, blasting our favourite songs at the time and at some point we even introduced a strobe light to the scene. We'd move furniture to have more room to dance and practice any new dance from music videos. It's a strange feeling to think back to being able to do certain things with significantly less pain and more ability to now knowing I am unable to do the things I used to do not so long ago. Losing my ability to dance and paint my toenails are just some of the things I wish endometriosis didn't steal from me in the dead of the night.

Despite the many ways endometriosis has stolen from me, I have had the privilege of choosing other ways to socialise, live, explore, experience and adventure. I have been able to build relationships with people who are kind, considerate and inclusive – friends who understand my limitations and are willing to compromise. I've found ways to enjoy music and dance without having to go to a club. I have explored unconventional ways of communing with others in ways that are comfortable for me. I am lucky to have been able to figure out different things to do for fun that suited my capabilities, like going to brunch, exploring tea tastings or champagne tastings, cooking with others, binge watching shows with delicious food and snacks, going to markets and even travelling. I have decided what works for me, and I no longer feel the urge to cause harm to myself in an attempt to do things I know I cannot do. I no longer have people around me who are unwilling to compromise. Asking for help from people who care about me has also become easier for me and less overwhelming. Endometriosis is a thief of mobility, pain-free days and overall health but I get to decide how much I want it to control and limit me. I decide what works for me in collaboration with my body and mind, but I will not let a disease make or break my sense of agency and freedom.

The waiting game

ON 24 MARCH 2020 I was scheduled for a check-up and final preparation appointment before my third surgery for endometriosis at Tygerberg Hospital. The day before President Cyril Ramaphosa announced that we would be heading for a hard lockdown for three weeks because of the mysterious COVID-19 pandemic. I didn't know what was to come and honestly just assumed that it would be contained within three weeks and surgeries and procedures scheduled would continue. My phone rang on 23 March. It was the administration department from the hospital to let me know that they didn't think it was a good idea for me to come in for my check-up. The woman on the phone sounded panicked. 'It's just that our hands are full and, honestly, it could be a risk for you to come to the hospital, we don't fully understand how the virus is spread.'

I tried to convince her to let me come in so I could have my surgery. I remember saying to her, almost pleading, 'But I have been waiting to have my surgery for over a year now. I was assured that I would be on a list as a matter of urgency, I can't wait – the pain is killing me!'

The woman sounded sympathetic and said, 'I understand, Ms Dirks, and I really am sorry but this is out of my hands and we are only taking on absolute emergencies right now. I will get back to you as soon as we have a handle on the situation and can start working on our elective bunch of surgeries.'

I sighed in annoyance as we hung up the phone, I said aloud, 'Emergencies? So, what is my condition? Just not serious at all?'

My symptoms not only persisted but worsened over the year. I had noticed significant left leg pain, and trouble walking. I had intense constipation, which I already knew meant that there was a chance my uterus and other reproductive organs had adhered to my bowel again, pulling it down and creating issues with bowel movements. I was still experiencing horribly painful, long and heavy menstrual cycles, passing blood clots the size of my palm. I started having frequent urinary tract infections, causing flank pain, difficulty passing urine, fever and nausea. I battled with severe fatigue and required naps daily in order to function.

Mentally, I was in a difficult space because I was feeling so unwell and in so much pain that I felt depressed and anxious. Chronic pain persisted and worsened; my lower back pain, pelvic pain, nerve pain, headaches and pain radiating down my back into my buttocks all became unbearable. I even noticed new pain in places I hadn't had issues before. I often experienced discomfort and sharp, aching pains when urinating and having bowel movements. Even more worrying, two days before I was scheduled to fly to Johannesburg for my big move, I had one of the most painful menstrual cycles I had ever had. This was on 18 January 2021. The pain was blinding, even on really strong pain killers. I felt like my body was being torn apart internally. I tried to get to bed early, with a hot water bottle, eager for some respite. I must have been asleep by 8:30 pm latest before being woken up at midnight by the feeling of my pelvis violently pulling and contracting. I had been in a foetal position in bed, digging my nails into my body, trying not to scream bloody murder. It was weird, considering I had been on medication to stop my period. I tried to take some pain medication and sleep it off, hoping the following day would be better. I shot up in bed with severe pain, sharp, like my insides were being ripped apart. I started sweating profusely from the pain.

I tried to get up and go to the bathroom, suspecting it may be a blood clot that needed to pass. I staggered my way through the dark to the bathroom, holding my abdomen. I sat down and noticed a drenched pad and blood gushing out of me. I held my belly and cried out as the pain worsened. My body seemed to be pushing without my consent.

Suddenly the pain intensified, then mellowed when I heard a loud plop into the toilet bowl. It caught me by surprise since blood clots are usually lighter in weight and don't make a loud noise. I called out for my mom, who came, screaming 'What happened?!' I tried to explain I had passed something as my mom tried to help me get up. I was hoping she would be able to identify the strange creature I had just birthed, but she was as mystified as I was. She grabbed some rubber gloves, a skewer and her phone to take photos to show the doctors.

Mom fished the large, fleshy, almost fibrous, muscle-like textured creature out and tried to make sense of it. It was covered in blood but didn't look familiar at all. I panicked, wondering if I had just lost an organ. It was in the early days of the pandemic, hospitals were overwhelmed and focusing on COVID-19 patients and, without medical aid, I knew I would not be a priority. I decided that my options were slim so I decided to dial a doctor friend and hope that she could at least confirm that it was not an organ and that I was okay. My friend responded with a bunch of shocked emojis after I had sent her the gory photos. She was unable to identify what she was looking at and insisted I go to a hospital. I reminded her I didn't have medical aid and she sighed heavily knowing how busy government hospitals were at the time and told me to monitor myself. She said to look out for more intense bleeding, fever, fatigue or just generally feeling unwell and told me to go to the trauma section of the closest hospital if I experienced any 'new' symptoms. I threw on two overlapping night pads and went back to bed. I didn't have five days to deal with the government hospitals and shitty healthcare; I had to get on a plane and live my dream in Jozi.

I arrived in Johannesburg like a character out of *West Side Story*, bright-eyed and bushy tailed. I was in the City of Gold, with my dream job secured, a spacious two-bedroom apartment and a community who cared for me. I was elated. Nothing was going to stop me. I daydreamed about how unstoppable and driven I would be.

'You are going to make change here,' I whispered to myself at the airport. Strutting like I hadn't just had another traumatic event wherein my endo tried to unalive me.

I vowed to myself that since my new job came with medical aid, I would make use of it as soon as I could and see an endometriosis specialist. Given how my symptoms seemed to have worsened, I knew I would likely need another surgery if I had any hope of returning to 'normal'. I figured that taking care of my health would only benefit my career and the work I was doing by giving me the ability to do my day-to-day tasks more easily. During my interview, I had informed my new employers that I had severe endometriosis and would require reasonable accommodation, which they seemingly had no issues with. They let me know they were a compassionate, inclusive space and that they were considerate of disabled people since they were a mental health non-profit organisation. I was elated and, for the first time in my career, I felt like I was in a position and organisation wherein – despite my disability and chronic illness – I could soar just like everyone else.

I started researching good endometriosis specialists in the Gauteng region. I would read up on each doctor, look at their websites, reviews and even scour endometriosis support groups for information on doctors. I had been so traumatised, abused and neglected in the public healthcare system for years and felt so disempowered since I could never truly advocate for myself. So, I dedicated myself to finding a kind, compassionate doctor with a dedication to treating endometriosis. I was naturally weary and anxious about doctors who were white, but surprisingly I was even more cautious of women doctors because an enormous amount of abuse I experienced was at the hands of women. I had started therapy a few months prior and used the skills I learned in therapy to advocate for myself, ask questions, ask for clarity and make sure the doctor was a good fit for me and my needs.

The doctor turned out to be a middle-aged Dutch man named Dr Blaauw. He had a thick accent, big build and infectious smile. He was attentive, concerned for me while simultaneously letting me know how serious and severe my stage and type of endometriosis was. For the first time ever, I had a doctor who listened to me about issues all my doctors before had either laughed off, scoffed at or blatantly ignored. He was expressive and even considerate of my budget affirming that, 'I do this because I want you to feel better.'

My new doctor even noticed that I had some difficulty walking due to nerve issues just by watching me walk into his office. He examined the level of strength in each leg and insisted I go for a nerve conduction test to check my nerve function in my left leg and foot. He was thorough and even searched for my medical records from the government hospitals in Cape Town where I had formerly been treated.

Based on the results of an MRI, which showed nerve issues because of endometriosis lesions in their proximity, including close to my spine and other vital organs, even covering my utero-sacral ligaments and nerves responsible for bladder and bowel functioning, my doctor decided that operating would be necessary and that we shouldn't wait too long.

He was open and frank with me. 'I want you to know, we cannot make it go away completely. The surgery will help, but it has limitations; you have really bad endometriosis.'

I nodded and held back tears because I knew this already but hearing it from a doctor who cared just felt different.

He continued, with a furrowed brow, holding a stack of my medical notes. "There are also risks of operating due to how bad your endometriosis is. It would likely be a long surgery – let's say maybe five hours. And because of where the endometriosis is, if we remove it in certain areas, it could affect your bladder and bowels so we can't be aggressive. Okay?'

I nodded again and said, 'Okay, I understand…'

It felt as if someone had punched me in the chest – I felt sheer dread and fear – and the room suddenly seemed too bright and too cold. My specialist suggested a few dates for surgery and told me to speak with my workplace. I would be scheduled for a keyhole surgery and up and going in two weeks according to my doctor. The reasonably accommodating workplace suddenly didn't seem so accommodating, but nonetheless I needed my surgery.

Since my family was in Cape Town, my friends rallied around me and my mom decided to come to Johannesburg a few days after I had surgery. I was nervous and anxious. I tried to look at the silver lining and remind myself that I needed the surgery. Leading up to it, I celebrated my 25th birthday with a few friends, and celebrated my life. I had a strange feeling that my life would never be the same again but I tried not to be negative and just keep going.

On the day of my birthday, 6 April, I had my nails done and headed over to my friend Jamil's home. Since it was a weekday, I had nothing much planned aside from just pure relaxation and some time with my friend – after all, on Saturday, I would be going all out. I walked into Jamil's beautiful home, filled with books, plants and an array of incense. I was met with the mouth-watering smell of something good cooking in the kitchen.

Jamil hurried over to greet me: 'Salaam! Happy birthday, baby! I am cooking steak, lemony garlicky sauteed broccoli, and some roasted potatoes. And we have to pop a bottle of Champagne!'

I was so grateful. 'My favourite food, drinks and good company?!' What more could I ask for. Life was good. On Saturday, I was showered with gifts, hugs and flowers. I was intentional about spending the day laughing, singing, eating and embracing my community. I didn't know what to expect from the surgery and I wanted to make sure I ate life.

We lit candles to thank the higher power for our lives, and to light the path for those who had just departed due to COVID complications like the beloved Dr Sindi van Zyl who had impacted us all so profoundly by living unapologetically. We played the song 'Little Blue Girl' by Black Motion, in her honour, because she loved it. She was also the Queen of Champagne and MCC so we had to pop a bottle in her memory. We shared stories while sitting on the floor just because we wanted to and laughed rhythmically.

I twerked and said, 'I better be able to do this twice as well post-surgery.'

Everyone laughed and Jamil said, 'Not even pain could stop you from shaking your ass and dropping it low!'

My guests ate my cooking like it was laced with an addictive drug, and I even got extra containers because who doesn't want a skhfatin? We listened to 'Jikijela' by Thandiswa Mazwai and something in me shifted; I swayed to her voice, smiling, knowing that the only certainty in life is that we will all die.

'When I die, this is one of the songs I want played at the memorial.'

I suspect everyone was tipsy enough to nod and not seem alarmed, or maybe just as I accepted death to be a fact of life, maybe they did too.

The scent of death lingered in the air

SURGERY DAY – 17 APRIL – soon came around. In the race to get to the hospital on time, I had completely forgotten that I had set up candles next to my statue of Mother Mary, impepho and a rosary. I quickly ran over in the dim light, knelt in front of the lit candle and impepho, and started to clap my cupped hands together. 'Thokoza bo gogo nabo mkhulu,' I said, inviting my ancestors with good intentions for my life to intercede on my behaviour, to pray and ensure I would be well.

I started to pray Our Father and Hail Mary, asking for my surgery to go smoothly. 'I want to be able to recover and continue to do meaningful work,' I petitioned.

As I opened my eyes, I noticed my green aventurine pendulum glistening in the light of the candle. 'Why not?' I thought to myself. I was slightly afraid – I didn't know what the pendulum would foreshadow – but I picked it up anyway in a hurry. I decided to ask a few questions while swinging it back and forth. 'Will everything go well with my surgery?'

I watched the pendulum swing and waited for it to settle, the response was loud; it swung left and right like someone shaking their head no. I brushed it off and tried again in a different way. 'Will this surgery be easy?' Again I watched it swing around and settle on a left to right swing saying no. 'Ag whatever,' I thought to myself. 'It's just a bunch of nonsense,' I convinced myself. I said another prayer for protection and healing before putting out the candles and impepho. I grabbed my rosary – I didn't want to forget it on my way out.

My surgery was scheduled for first thing in the morning. The hospital looked vacant when I arrived before 6 am. It was still dark outside and unseasonably chilly. I walked in and waited for the admin staff to check in. While I waited, I updated my family and sent them a photo of a sign in the empty reception area, above a set of plush blue chairs, which read 'voted best hospital…' I don't recall what they were best at but it made me feel less anxious for the moment. I had a bag packed, with my blue mask to keep COVID at bay, holding a stack of papers. I was quickly ushered to the ward I would be in. It was right next to the nurse's station with four beds, three of which had already been filled. The fourth bed was closest to the door.

'Can you please put your bag away in your locker and change into the hospital gown on the bed. I am going to fetch some paperwork I need for you to fill out, ne?' the nurse asked me quickly.

I nodded and looked over at the white and blue gown neatly folded into a square on the bed. I sat down on the bed and looked at the room. It was spacious and not as tight as a big government hospital ward. It looked older than I expected for a private hospital, the paint was an ugly beige-peach shade that screamed 1962, the curtains were old and worn, and the equipment and side tables looked just as dated as the ones I had used before.

The nurse, a tall woman, with long braids she had put up in a bun, came over to go through the paperwork with me. She was in a rush to get me ready because I was first on the list.

The porter arrived to take me to the operating room, and I was told I needed to hand over my glasses. As I was wheeled to the operating room, the hospital looked like blurs of beige, blues, reds and greens without my glasses. Faces melted into a shade of brown and the waiting room looked blurry too. I tried to calm myself down by reminding myself that surgery would start at 8 am and I would be out by 1 pm, ready to start healing so I could go back home to my life. The staff came to introduce themselves to me before I was wheeled into the operating room. It was bright, and filled with equipment and apparatus, nurses and other healthcare experts crowded around me. It was overwhelming being asked multiple questions by different people, all while others were starting to set things up on and around me. One person with dark hair was inserting a cannula into my left arm, while others tried to get the bed I arrived in aligned with the narrow, thin blue bed used during the surgery.

My doctor smiled and said, 'Don't worry, it's okay, we have people here to help with different parts of the surgery because of your type of endometriosis. Just take deep breaths.'

I nodded and managed to smile while being shifted onto the operating table. The nurse looked down at me and said, 'Don't worry, my baby, I will be with you the whole time, even when you wake up.'

I squeezed her hand and said thank you.

A dark-haired man put a mask over my face and told me to breathe normally, as he counted down… '10, 9, 8,' I felt my eyelids get heavy and then nothing at all.

I woke up briefly in the waiting area, feeling sore and groggy. I had had a few surgeries before, but this felt different, I couldn't keep my eyes open for long and felt nauseous. I felt my mouth fill with saliva, preparing to throw up. I motioned to the nurse that I was going to throw up. She held a throw away kidney-shaped bowl to my mouth just in time. The nurse sounded so far away as she said something like, 'Hai shame… it's the anaesthesia making you naar.'

I dosed off again before feeling a burning pain across my abdomen. I opened my eyes but they felt so heavy, things were still blurry but, as we passed a window, it looked like it was still dark outside. I thought to myself that they probably ran into an issue and couldn't operate hence it still looked dark. I mustered up enough strength, with my eyes still closed, to ask the nurse beside me what time it was currently. 'Uh… it is 8:30 pm now, my dear,' she said.

I was surprised but too out of it to really react.

I woke up in a room by myself. It seemed almost sterile, all white, with a giant glass section where you'd think a wall should be. I looked around me trying to focus my eyes and make sense of my surroundings but my body revolted against the slightest movement. I felt like a semi-truck had hit me. I groaned loudly in pain. I had a cannula in my nose, secured tightly under my chin. My bed seemed to be really high up for some reason, with both metal safety bars up – in case I decided to move my aching body, I guess. Through the glass windows I could see medical personnel watching me, making notes and checking medical equipment. They were whispering amongst themselves. I turned my head and noticed a massive piece of machinery with pipes coming out of it attached to my body, alongside a bunch of monitors. My urethra spasmed in unison with my groaning,

'I must have a catheter inserted, I can't stand the feeling of fiery hell!' I thought to myself.

I still couldn't see a thing, which added to the feeling of confusion. A chubby nurse in a white top approached me to check if I was okay. She seemed to be smiling but my eyesight is so poor she could very well have just been baring her teeth.

'You're awake, sleepyhead! Finally… My name is Sr Nonhlanhla, how are you feeling?' she said in a calming and pleasant tone, as she rubbed my hand.

I still felt disorientated but she made me feel safe. 'Sister, do you know where my glasses and phone are please? I can't see and I need to speak to my mom.'

She continued to rub my hand and said, 'Yes, I will call the security to bring it to you, okay?'

I smiled. 'Sister, what happened to me? Where am I?' I asked in almost a whisper.

She looked at me and explained that there were complications. 'So, you are currently in the ICU, your surgery was very complicated, and the doctors ran into a few complications so the surgery took much longer than expected. Your doctor will explain what happened. Okay?'

I paused for a few seconds and groaned in pain. 'Okay, but why am I in ICU though?'

Sr Nonhlanhla poured some water into a small glass for me while answering my question.

'Well, sisi, your surgery was 12 hours long, so the doctors felt it was best to send you to ICU so we can monitor you and make sure you are okay.'

I nodded. Pain ripped through my body in waves. Sr Nonhlanhla must have noticed the pain on my face because she said, 'Let me look at your folder and see when we can give you more pain meds in your drip and a morphine injection ne?'

I nodded and said please.

Sr Nonhlanhla said I was just in time to get my next dose of pain killers. She came back with a metal cart with medicine bottles, cleaning supplies, cotton wool, syringes and everything in between, the security tailing her, a mountain of a man in a black and blue uniform, with a serious demeaner. He was holding a red pouch with a zip and a small padlock. He looked at the sticker on the pouch and on my folder before carefully looking at me. 'Okay,' he said, satisfied that I was indeed the owner of the contents of the red pouch. He unlocked and unzipped the bag and handed me a box with my glasses. I eagerly put my glasses on so I could see the world semi clearly again. He handed me my phone and for some odd reason my hairband. I wasn't complaining because my hair was a poofy mess. I asked Sr Nonhlanhla if she could tie my hair up since moving my arms too much felt like torture. Before Serious Face Security left, he asked, 'Are you sure these are your belongings?' before requesting I sign a form stating I had received my things.

Sr Nonlanhla told me that if I wanted to call or text anyone, I should do so now. 'Once I give you your injection, you will be in lala land,' she said with a giggle.

I quickly let my family know I was okay and in ICU recovering while Sr Nonhlanhla changed out the empty bottle of pain killers attached to my drip with a full bottle. She added some meds for nausea and then prepared the injection.

'Which arm do you want it in? I can't do buttocks; your abdomen is too sore now to turn you.'

I agreed and quickly said 'No ways!' I couldn't imagine being turned on my side or belly so soon post-surgery when even tying my own hair hurt.

'We can do the right arm since you are on my right, sister,' I said.

The needle itself wasn't intimidating, it was a tiny syringe with a thin needle on the end. Sister cleaned my arm with an alcohol wipe, before counting down from three to give me my shot.

'That wasn't so bad!' I said, and she went, 'Yes, well, after having multiple incision sites in your stomach, this is easy peasy!'

While she put a piece of cotton wool attached to tape onto my arm, I felt myself drifting away. The medication was like a warm hug from a grandma. I felt the pain subside almost instantly while my eyes fluttered gently closed.

I heard light beeping noises, and people talking around me, but I tried to keep my eyes closed so as to not fully wake up just yet; I still felt loopy. The voices seemed to get closer and louder. I opened my eyes and realised the nurses were changing shifts and were doing a handover. They were apologetic for waking me, which was a lovely shift from my experiences at government hospitals where nurses would turn the bright florescent lights on at 4 am in the morning, while playing gospel music loudly on their phones, screaming across the ward to the other nurses while emptying urine bags.

A kind older woman wearing a navy blue doek came to my room with a food tray. 'I didn't get a selection from you, so I just chose this but you can tell me if you don't like it, mntanam,' she said as she lifted the heavy dark blue plastic cover. It was two slices of toast, two sausages, two fried eggs and some fried tomatoes. She had also added a small bowl of fresh fruit and a little box of apple juice.

I hadn't eaten for two days since I had had to do a bowel flush before surgery and I hadn't realised how hungry I was until the kind-faced woman uncovered the food and the aroma wafted through the air.

'This is perfect, thank you so much, mama, I am happy with this,' I said while smiling at her.

She also pulled out a big glass jug filled with water and ice, the jug's exterior dripping with giant water droplets to entice me. She moved the tray so it would be situated over my abdomen and helped me adjust myself and lift the back of the bed so I could be a more seated position.

I drank the water first. It felt heavenly. I tried not to chug but it was so refreshing. I tried to eat some of my food but, although I was hungry, my body was just not ready to hold a full meal. I nibbled on one slice of toast, some of the egg and a piece of the sausage before moving to eat the fruit. It was delicious and my first time receiving freshly cut up fruit in hospital, especially a variety of fruit. I drank more water and sucked on the ice to alleviate the nausea.

I asked the nurse how long I would be in ICU. 'Well, it was for observation, so it depends on your doctor. He will come see you a little bit later today and then he will decide.' I thanked her before she headed off to get my meds.

I took the time to take selfies because my face felt swollen. To my surprise it was indeed swollen; even my lips and eyes looked swollen. If I hadn't been in so much pain, I may have laughed at the sight of my own face. I felt tired and nodded off. As I slept lightly, the nurse changed my drips and I felt a prick in the arm as she administered my injection.

I was awoken by my endometriosis specialist standing over me, gently tapping me and saying, 'Hello, Nadine, how are you?'

I opened my eyes to see my doctor in a light blue shirt, with a pen clipped to his shirt pocket which had bled blue ink throughout the left side of the pocket. He went to view my folder while I tried to wake myself up properly. He seemed to be reading each page intensely.

'How are you feeling?' he prompted again while tilting his head sideways slightly and smiling.

'I'm okay, I think. Just in a lot of pain and confused because I am in ICU.'

His smile faded and his eyes looked serious. 'It was a lot more complicated than we thought. As you know with endometriosis, it is a very ugly disease because it often surprises you when you open a patient up. Your surgery was 12 hours long. The endometriosis was very extensive. It isn't good for you to be under anaesthesia for so long – it is stressful on the body and that is why I asked them to monitor you in ICU.'

I swallowed hard, suddenly feeling very emotional and alone. COVID protocols meant that I couldn't even see a familiar face because we couldn't have visitors.

'Okay, I understand. I know my endometriosis is severe and you had estimated five hours, but why was it 12 hours, doctor?'

Dr Blaauw came around the bed to my right side and explained what happened. 'We inserted a camera and found endometriosis everywhere. You had a frozen pelvis, the endometriosis was on your utero-sacral ligaments, nerves, at the base of your spine, around the bowel. There were also endometriomas, lesions and scar tissue present. The endometriosis even spread all the way to your kidneys. We ended up operating for 12 hours because it is a delicate process and we can't rush and it was a lot to remove.'

I struggled to keep up as my doctor recalled the 12-hour-long surgery to me. 'A frozen pelvis?' I interjected, I had never heard that term before and imagined a pelvis in a deep freezer. It didn't sound particularly medical to me.

Dr Blaauw answered, 'Oh! Uhm... okay, how do you say this,' he said aloud to himself. I could see the wheels spinning in his head.

'Well, because of the severity of your endometriosis, your pelvis is referred to as frozen because the reproductive organs and the structures surrounding it are kind of distorted, it doesn't look as it should, this is because endometriosis creates like an adhesive lesion and growths – which pulls your organs into unnatural positions. It caused fibrosis of the tissue as well, making it tough.'

I stared at him blankly, I couldn't really visualise what he was describing, it just sounded like a description for a tough cut of beef. He continued to explain how this affected the time it took to operate. 'Because your organs are not where they should be, it creates difficulties for us – we cannot follow normal surgical planes, which makes separating things and restoring anatomical placement tedious. It also increases the risk of accidentally injuring vital organs.'

Damn, so much for my former doctors saying, 'Endometriosis won't kill you'. 'This sounds pretty life threatening to me,' I thought.

Dr Blaauw continued to express what he had found. 'We also found that your ovaries and pouch of Douglas were completely obliterated by adhesions. We had to remove extensive endometriosis plaques from both ovaries, both ureters, particularly your left ureter, your anterior rectum, both utero-sacral ligaments, posterior vagina as well as endometriosis tissue of the sacral plexus.'

It sounded like a list of gibberish to me. I didn't have the energy to talk about how awful the situation was, all I wanted to know were three things: 1. When can I go to a normal ward? 2. When can my catheter be removed? 3. When can I go home?

Dr Blaauw told me I could go to a ward later that afternoon, my catheter could be removed in the ward and I would need to be monitored a little bit longer before he could give me an idea as to when I could go home. 'This was very serious, you had endometriosis around your ureter on the left side, it was causing issues because it was narrowing the ureter. We removed it but because of all the nerves involved, we have to see if you can pass urine and have bowel movements on your own before we can consider discharging you.'

I tried not to focus on the kidney issues; I just needed to get stronger and go home, I told myself. Then I could fall apart about how traumatising it was. 'Okay, doctor, that sounds easy enough,' I said in response to urinating and defecating on my own.

Dr Blaauw looked at me quite seriously, his face a deep red. I couldn't tell whether he was getting hot or if he were nervous and concerned for me. He said, 'It may not be that easy, sometimes after these surgeries, the nerves can be lazy or damaged on one side; we need to evaluate that and manage the situation. When you do go to the bathroom, opening the tap in the basin could help you urinate because of the sound of the water, okay? You will try it?' I smiled and let him know I understood and would try to open the tap before urinating.

When I returned to the ward I had initially been assigned to, it was dusk. The old woman in the left corner was fast asleep and snoring gently. The young woman next to me, with thick-framed purple glasses, was watching TV with earphones on and the other woman across from me had just gotten up, wheeling her drip along with her to the bathroom.

The friendly nurse who had checked me in before surgery beamed when she saw me. 'Where have you been? We've been waiting for you. All your things are still here,' she said cheerfully.

I smiled, slightly confused and wondering why no one informed the ward that I was in ICU.

'I was in ICU, but I am back now. Didn't they tell you?' I enquired.

She looked at me, still smiling, and winked, 'They did! I am just playing with you!'

I breathed a sigh of relief, settling into the room; it felt a little lighter than ICU. I told myself. 'It's okay, just a few more days and you'll be home with Mommy and Jamil, and then can focus on recovering fully.' My good friend, mentor and publisher Nadia was meant to stop by on Sunday with a few things I had forgotten. It was unlike her to not show up. I figured when the nurse returned I would ask her if Nadia had stopped by and dropped off my things while I was in ICU – it was possible I missed her. I checked my phone in the meantime, wading through dozens of calls, texts and emails in search of communication from Nadia, but she hadn't sent anything new.

The nurse, who I had learned was called MaLisebo, came back smiling. 'My baby!' she announced as she came towards me with a smile, and a white plastic apron covering her uniform. 'Is there anything you want? Have you been able to wash at all since surgery?'

I was grateful she asked since I wasn't sure how it worked. I was never bathed in government hospitals before: I either had to do it myself with incisions, tubes, IVs and pain, or my mom would bath me in my hospital bed. This time, I was by myself and my mom couldn't assist me and I knew I couldn't go and try and bath myself – I was in a lot of pain, still wearing a catheter and I had a drain attached across my lower abdomen. I looked at her face, trying to assess if I could ask for assistance.

'MaLisebo, could I please be assisted with washing myself and brushing my teeth please? I haven't been able to bathe or brush my teeth since the morning of my surgery,' I asked her.

'Of course! Let me go get a few things.' MaLisebo started to close my curtains before she left. 'You can undress as far as you can, if you want to do it yourself.'

Before she could leave, I asked, 'MaLisebo, can you please check if my friend Nadia was here or if she left anything here for me?'

She nodded and smiled.

I tried to see if I could get the hospital gown off, but it proved difficult over my arm with an IV attached. MaLisebo returned with a few things on a cart. First, she handed me the white plush hospital towel, a fresh hospital gown, a sanitary pad, alcohol pads, medical supplies and a metal bowl with warm water and soap.

'I checked for you, nana, your friend wasn't here yet,' she said as she readied herself to assist me.

She gently used the alcohol pads to wipe any crusty blood off of my body, before squeezing the excess water out of a white face cloth and washing my face thoroughly. 'Let me wipe your eyes, I can see some crusty bits.'

I smiled.

As she finished the right eye she said, 'There you go! O motle man!'

MaLisebo almost made me forget why I was there, she was just so warm and jovial; it was an easy distraction. She washed my entire body gently, and then asked if I wanted to wash my own vulva. I took the cloth, rang it out and cleaned myself gently around the catheter. MaLisebo had started to dry me off in the meantime, after which she asked me if she could assist with moisturiser and deodorant. She put on my gown and said, 'There you go. You probably feel like a new person now.' And I did

'Thank you, MaLisebo,' I said. 'When can my catheter be removed? It is so uncomfortable and even painful when I move.'

She rubbed my hand and said sorry to me. 'I can't remove it until your doctor says so. I will write it down in your file though and ask him, okay? I will just go clean the tray and then I will come back and clean your wounds, and I will check if the catheter is in correctly. It is almost time for your meds.'

I nodded. I had hated catheters since my first surgery – it is incredibly painful for me, although many medical professionals have told me it was just my imagination and that catheters are not meant to hurt. I was grateful that MaLisebo seemed like a kind person, but she also seemed to listen to me and believe my word, which was refreshing.

She returned ten minutes later with another cart. This time she had my medications, syringes, alcohol pads, saline, cotton wool, wound dressings and various other medical apparatus. I tensed up looking at the tray, I didn't want to deal with intense pain and a nurse in a rush like I was used to. MaLisebo immediately started cleaning a glass bottle to go onto my drip. She worked almost mechanically and, before I knew it, the bottle was upside and dripping down into the tube. MaLisebo used a scrolling motion on an orange switch of sorts to release the medication. I watched the little droplets fall into the reservoir, inevitably ending up in my bloodstream.

'Perfect. I wanted to start some of the pain medication before I set up and clean wounds and check your catheter. It will kick in soon.'

I smiled at her and thanked her as she changed her blue gloves again and started to pour saline into a kidney dish.

After dinner – a hearty helping of beef stew, rice and veggies – I got my medication for the evening and drifted off, wondering when I would be discharged. But first I needed the damn catheter removed!

I struggled to get comfortable in the bed; the light from the nurses' station beamed into the room. The old lady on the left side of the room across from me coughed loudly and frequently and it sounded awful.

During a respiratory pandemic, the coughing made me really nervous, especially since she was not wearing a mask and the windows were closed. I tried to put a mask over my nasal cannula and tried to force my eyes shut, longing for the morning so I could see my doctor and ask when I could leave.

My mom would also be arriving in Johannesburg in the morning and I just tried to hold on until then. I was worried about Nadia. It wasn't like her to not show up or not say anything either. I decided to send her a quick message on WhatsApp to update her on my hospital stay and surgery woes. I ended off by asking her, 'Are you okay? I checked with the nurses to see if you were here. They said no. Don't worry if you couldn't make it, I just wanna make sure you're okay.' I figured she would reply in the morning.

I woke up around 4 am when someone gently tapped me awake. I slowly opened my eyes to an unfamiliar face. It was a thin woman wearing a black scarf, in a blue uniform. She introduced herself and let me know she was from Pathcare and needed to take my blood for testing so that the results were ready for when my doctor came in. I stuck my right arm out and made a fist, nodding off. I felt the cold wetness and strong smell from the alcohol pad, a sharp pinch and the plaster being slapped on, while she held down and applied pressure onto my arm. I had never had blood work done post-surgery before. Everything seemed so new, I wondered if it was because I had never been in ICU before. When I woke up next, I heard my mom's voice and opened my eyes just as she appeared beside me. Mom was wearing a light blue floral top and a pair of blue jeans. She asked me how I was feeling, and if I had seen my doctor yet. She looked worried. I told her I was okay but we would wait for my doctor to pop by. In the meantime, I filled my mom in about the surgical difficulties and the 12-hour-long surgery.

'What!? 12 hours? Straight? I have never heard of a surgery that long before.'

She was especially dumbfounded about my kidney issues. 'I just don't understand how it spread to your kidneys but also it is shocking how these other asses didn't notice this before! No wonder you had to go to ICU.'

Mom gently started to comb my hair for me, while I lay down.

'Mommy, it's so weird. Nadia was meant to stop by yesterday and bring me a few things but she didn't show up and didn't send a message or anything! It is so unlike her,' I said while my mom twisted my hair into a bun.

'That is unusual for her... maybe try and message her and see if she's okay?' my mom suggested.

I suddenly remembered that in my pain medication stupor, I had messaged her the night before. I checked my phone and noticed a reply from her. 'Hello my little chicken. I am so glad you are out of the woods. I'm so sorry I didn't show up as promised. Not feeling my best, I think I have a cold. I didn't want to risk making you sick. I am going to my doctor today. I will update you. Love you mean it,' her message read, I read it to my mom.

'Well, that makes sense, shame. You don't want to make people sick when they are recovering from surgery. I hope she feels okay soon,' my mom said as Dr Blaauw walked into the room.

'Hello, Nadine,' he said to me, smiling.

'Is this your mother?' he asked, reaching his hand out to introduce himself.

Dr Blaauw was wearing a crisp white shirt, no ink stains yet. He shared some of my surgical details with my mom, as he put his glasses on to read from my hospital file.

'Okay, good,' he said while nodding. 'You can have your catheter removed today; your bloodwork looks fine. If you are mobilising and able to urinate and have a bowel movement on your own then we can look at sending you home tomorrow.'

I was ecstatic to hear that I could go home so soon.

'Can you walk?' he asked me.

I was eager to get up and walk so he could see I was mobile. My mom and Dr Blaauw helped me up, I slipped on my dark blue bedroom slippers and walked around the room as Dr Blaauw watched me. He seemed impressed and laughed in excitement.

'Your mobility seems better, huh? Your dropped left leg isn't as severe, it seems. This is good, it is because we removed the endometriosis around your utero-sacral ligaments, nerves and other areas. How do you feel?' he asked.

'I think it is too soon for me to say because I am still in pain, but my left foot does seem to be slightly more agile.'

He nodded and advised that I mobilise and remember to open a tap when I urinate to help the process.

'If all goes well, you can go home tomorrow.'

He called the nurse to tell her that my drain and catheter could be removed. I was relieved as this meant I was well on my way to healing and getting on with my life as planned.

A young nurse I had never seen before came to assist me. She was tall and had burgundy-framed glasses.

'So, what would you like to do first, sisi? The catheter or the drain?'

Without hesitation I said, 'Definitely the catheter!' After all, I had been waiting for this moment forever.

I tried to relax and look at the ceiling as the nurse prepared the tools she needed and put on her blue gloves. 'Please try to relax,' she said, as she moved my thigh further away to give her more room.

I winced and felt myself tense up, and just like that it was over. I immediately felt more comfortable.

The nurse said, 'Okay, that's over! Now for the drain.'

I had never had a drain removed before so I didn't know what to expect. I examined the tools and saw a scalpel and started getting nervous. She changed her gloves, set up a little bowl with saline in it, some gauze, the scalpel and some wound dressings.

'Just relax, I am going to tell you when to take a big breath in and out when I pull it out, I am going to cut the end of the stitches very gently with the scalpel.'

I nodded, trying to relax, which as you can imagine given the circumstances was no walk in the park. She grabbed some gauze and dipped it into the saline before wiping the little wound and stitches on the left side of my swollen abdomen, it felt so cold yet refreshing. She picked up the scalpel, face up, and gently cut the stitches in one swift motion, before putting it back down in her tray. She grabbed some kind of big tweezers and told me, 'Okay, when I say go, you start to breathe in as deeply as possible and then exhale. Okay?'

I nodded. 'Okay, got it.'

'Go!' she said.

I breathed in deeply, focusing on my breath, and exhaled. Before I knew it, she was holding a thin flexible thing she had just removed from my body.

'That's the drain?' I said in disbelief.

'Yes, it is, it's called a pencil drain.'

She smiled and cleaned the wound one last time before adding a small wound dressing to it.

I drank glass after glass of cold water from the jug besides my bed, excited to finally urinate on my own and head home at last.

The day dragged by. I watched YouTube videos on my phone to pass the time. When I finally went to pee, it took some time for a stream to start, and I had forgotten to open the taps while I urinated to trick my brain. It seemed uneventful and so did the bowel movement which I reported to the nurses enthusiastically, making sure they wrote it down in my folder. I was not going to be stuck in hospital for a moment longer than necessary.

I woke up in the early hours of the morning to the sound of nurses getting ready to change shifts. I reminded myself, 'Just a few more hours before you can go home, and sleep in your own bed.' Soon after the shift change, Dr Blaauw came by and studied my file carefully, with his glasses resting on the very tip of his nose.

'Ah, Nadine,' he said smiling, 'it seems all went well. You've been walking, and been able to urinate and have bowel movements on your own. That's great.' He grinned.

I smiled broadly and said, 'Yes! I have been doing well, doctor,' hoping he wouldn't insist on keeping me over for an additional night for monitoring.

'Okay, you can arrange for someone to pick you up, you can leave today.'

I couldn't be more pleased. I let my mom and Jamil know, and they hurried over to fetch me. It felt so bizarre walking into my apartment building foyer in a nightdress and some slippers in broad daylight, but I didn't have many options. The lights seemed so much warmer than the hospital lights. I was grateful to sit down on my blue couch, with a pink hot water bottle behind my back, my mom doting on me and making my favourite meals. It felt so comforting to have my mom and Jamil there, and listening to them joke and talk about everything they'd got up to while my mom was visiting from Cape Town.

I felt relatively okay, aside from major swelling in the abdomen – the pain came and went – and I had to remember to take my medication on time. My mom helped me bath myself, using a waskom because I couldn't get in the shower and risk wetting my wounds. Mom had to help me undress too since I couldn't lift my arms to take tops off by myself without stretching my abdominal muscles too much. I had been given supplies by the hospital to clean and take care of the wounds.

'Do you need help, what must I do?' my mom asked me as I sat on my bed, propped up by a mountain of pillows, holding the wound dressing.

'Yes please, I need to clean it with the saline, and then add gauze to absorb any liquid and then the dressing.'

My mom nodded and got to work. She sanitised her hands before taking the old dressing off and discarding it, and then sanitised again. She gently tapped the incision areas with gauze soaked in saline. 'Tell me if its sore,' she said, without looking up, focusing on the incisions before adding a thin layer of Supiroban and covering it with a wound dressing. She helped me put on some warm pyjamas she had gotten for me and helped me get comfortable in bed. I took my pain killers and tried to get some sleep. I felt restless and couldn't seem to get comfortable. I tried to turn slightly on my side but my abdomen just felt distended and more painful than before. I thought I may be constipated and got up to got to the bathroom but nothing happened.

My mom and Jamil were still sitting in the living room, talking about the British royals and how much they both detested Prince Charles. I decided maybe if I tried to slowly walk it would help reset my bowels.

'Are you okay?' my mom asked when I walked into the living room.

'I think so, my tummy feels weird like I'm constipated or something.'

Mom and Jamil laughed lightly in relief, before offering to make me some tea, hoping it would settle my stomach. I went back to bed with my tea and fell asleep gently.

There were complications

I WOKE UP WITH THE MORNING light streaming in, feeling strange, like something wasn't quite right. Every day in recovery should become easier to manage but this seemed to be the opposite – I felt weaker and in more pain. I also didn't have much of an appetite and felt nauseous.

My mom started to worry because I seemed to be declining and decided to call Dr Blaauw and let him know I was not doing well. He asked my mom to bring me in for an additional CT scan the following day and ordered me to take it easy in the meantime. I worried about the CT scan, knowing my medical aid wouldn't cover it as an outpatient service and that I would need to pay at least R1500 up front. I worried about being able to afford the medical bills and just the cost of living while being unwell. I tried to eat a few spoonfuls and at least still felt thirsty so I found myself hydrating at least. I slept for most of the day, while my mom busied herself around my apartment.

I woke up in the early evening feeling worse. I felt clammy and feverish; the pain in my abdomen was so much worse. I asked my mom to call an ambulance as I lay in bed unable to move much. My mom looked worried and panicked while she tried to call an ambulance, standing at the window in my bedroom as if she could will them to show up. A man and a woman showed up around 30 minutes later and took my vitals and told us, 'From our end, your vitals are stable, you are still awake and alert so we don't think taking you to hospital right now is the right move.' They urged my mom to get in touch with Dr Blaauw first thing in the morning, which she would since I had to show up for the CT scan.

The following morning, I had declined even more. I felt weak and I was in a lot of pain. Walking was quite painful and I still couldn't really eat. At the hospital I felt like people were staring at me, noticing that I seemed unwell. It could have been in my head. A porter came to assist my mom with a wheelchair given my condition. My mind is blank on what happened during the CT scan, but I distinctly remembering needing blood tests done at the hospital. The porter wheeled me to the pathology office, while my mom walked next to me. I could sense her anxiety.

I got up from the wheelchair and all of a sudden the pain in the right side of my abdomen intensified; I just wanted to get it over with so I could go home and rest. My mom went to the counter and handed over my folder to a lovely woman named Ayanda who remembered my name from previous blood tests. She quickly got up and asked me to follow her, which I did, very slowly. We got to a small cubicle, where I sat down while Ayanda looked at the list of blood tests she needed to collect.

As she prepared her station, she looked over at me and said, 'You don't look well, shame, are you in pain?'

I nodded, feeling like talking would worsen my pain.

She looked at me with concern and said, 'You should ask your doctor to admit you because then at least they can monitor you and give you stronger meds.'

I smiled and said that I would ask him, even though I knew I really didn't want to be admitted again. The pain was so blinding that being admitted didn't seem like such a bad idea.

My mom and I headed home in an Uber that seemed to be taking forever. I asked my mom if she would make me some scrambled eggs when we got home so I could take my meds and go back to sleep. I was hopeful that by the following day my doctor could let us know what the scan and blood tests revealed.

I ate the tiny bit of scrambled egg with some cranberry juice in bed, forcing myself so I could take my pain pills. After just a few bites, I started feeling nauseous and quickly grabbed my meds and drank them before the nausea took over. I then quickly passed out.

When I woke up, it was early evening again. The apartment was quiet – my mom seemed to be getting some rest herself. I felt awful, the pain was excruciating, my right side felt like it was being stabbed continuously. I felt like I needed to go to the bathroom so I steadied myself and slowly walked to the bathroom. I sat down on the toilet as sweat dripped down my entire body. The pain intensified as I suddenly projectile vomited remnants of scrambled eggs onto the bathroom floor. I shouted for my mom, feeling like I was unable to get up by myself. I felt hot and unwell.

My mom came running towards me, her facial expression scared me when she saw me – she looked terrified – I can't imagine what it looked like from her view. She jumped into action, cleaning the vomit and getting me back to my bed before calling the ambulance again. They seemed to take forever and I was losing consciousness. I felt hot in between experiencing chills and couldn't keep my eyes open. The pain was unbearable and like nothing I had ever felt before. My mom called my dad, who was back in Cape Town, and let him know what was going on while she stood by the window waiting for the ambulance. She kept talking to me to keep me awake and alert but it was a challenge. Every few minutes she'd say, 'Nadine ... kom nou, djy kannie slaapie.'

My mom tried calling the ambulance again in a panic but they were all the way in Midrand making their way to us. The ambulance arrived and I have no recollection as to what happened but I was put in the back of the vehicle, and the paramedic gave me a drip before we started our journey to the hospital. I looked for my mom in between falling in and out of consciousness, knowing I would die soon if something wasn't done. I needed to know my mom was with us on our way to the hospital.

I managed to coherently ask, 'Where is my mom? I am getting hot.'

'She's with us, in the front,' the paramedic responded before shouting. 'Please turn on the air conditioning!'

Even while not fully alert, I could feel each pothole because it caused pain to ripple throughout my body. I groaned in pain trying to figure out how far away we were from the hospital.

When we arrived at the trauma unit, I was immediately taken to the ward I had been in before. My mom was on the phone with my doctor who had received the results of my blood tests and scan. He told my mom, 'There seems to be some sort of infection and the scan shows that there may be a ureteric injury, hence the pain.'

The nurse, paramedic and my mom stayed in the ward with me. I felt thirsty and disorientated. I asked if I could have some water but the nurse said, 'We can't let you drink water, they will need to operate.' I was too out of it to understand and asked for some ice to suck on. She returned and gave me a cup with a few ice cubes. I begged for morphine while the doctor was on the phone with my mom.

'I am so sorry, ma, I can't just give you morphine,' the nurse said to me gently.

My mom asked the doctor if I could please have pain medication. My mom then handed the phone to the nurse who grabbed a pen and started to write down the medication in my folder. I was relieved when she returned with the medicine cart and started an antibiotic drip with paracetamol, and then gave me a morphine injection in my arm. For the first time, I had felt some relief.

The following morning, I was awoken by nurses preparing me for surgery. I was first on the list again so I needed to be taken to the operating room as soon as possible. I still felt out of it, but in slightly less pain – I suppose the pain medication and the drips were helpful. I felt extremely anxious, I was still recovering from my previous surgery and didn't know what the surgeons intended on doing. I felt worried about my finances because I would be out of work longer than I had discussed with my employer. I didn't know how much of the medical bills would be covered by my medical aid and my family was far away.

I let the nurses undress me and put me in a hospital gown for surgery while I lay in my hospital bed. One of the nurses asked me, 'Do you have any jewellery or hair pins in your hair? Do you have any dentures, or anything we need to remove before we take you down to theatre?'

I thought for a second and said, 'No, just my glasses.'

The nurse then asked me to take them off and give them to her to be put in a locker along with my phone. The porter arrived shortly after to take me down to the theatre. I hated not having my glasses with me – it added to my anxiety and fear of the unknown since I couldn't see much beyond shapes, shadowy figures and colours.

When we got to the theatre floor, a theatre nurse came by to check my paperwork, armband and to ask me a few questions, I guess to verify consent and to ensure I knew what I was there for. She held my folder and asked me, 'What is your name?'

I looked at her puzzled and said, 'Nadine Dirks.'

She nodded and ticked off a box on a list. 'Do you know what the doctors are doing today?' she asked.

'Uh ... I think they want to see what is causing the infection and pain and to fix something,' I said, unsure of the finer details since no one had discussed it with me at length.

'Okay, good. Doctor will be with you soon.'

I waited for the surgeons to show up. Without my glasses on, I tried to scan the shadowy faces in this massive, monochromic theatre filled with busy healthcare professionals. Everyone seemed to be wearing a green hat of sorts, scrubs and shoes with little disposable booties covering them.

Dr Blaauw arrived out of nowhere. 'Hi Nadine, are you ready? How do you feel?' he asked.

'Hi Doc, I guess I have to be ready, I am in a lot of pain, more than ever before.'

He nodded with a concerned look. 'Okay, so, I will be joined by a urologist who will be ready if we need any assistance with your ureter, and so on, so don't worry, you will be in good hands. We will also be looking at everything internally to make sure you are okay and we will find out which antibiotics are best for you. Hang in there.'

I nodded, too teary and drowsy to speak. Before I knew it, I was taken into theatre, surrounded by doctors and nurses introducing themselves to me. I was in too much pain so they decided to sedate me before attempting to move me from my hospital bed onto the operating table; I have never been so grateful.

Dr Blaauw noticed my distress and said, 'It's okay, we will get to the bottom of this, don't worry.'

I tried to smile and nod as the anaesthesiologist started to put me under. As he put the mask on my face, he said, 'Let's count from 3, okay?'

On the count of three I was already slipping away. According to surgical notes I was in theatre for five hours, and I was admitted to ICU again after an attempt to stent my left ureter was unsuccessful due to the damage done to it during the previous surgery. The scan I had done the day I was admitted again showed leakages from my ureter where 2 cm of the pipe had essentially started to die. The urologist had to immediately extend the existing incision from my previous surgery, essentially from hip to hip, to reimplant the healthy part of my ureter back into my bladder. Urine had seeped into my abdominal cavity, contributing to the sepsis. The doctors were also confronted with abscesses in my abdomen that needed to be removed, and my peritoneal cavity was 'extensively washed out with normal saline'.

I don't remember much of my healing journey in ICU apart from bits and pieces. The first few days were difficult: I had to keep the urine catheter in for 14 days this time to avoid overworking my healing ureter and I was still in a lot of pain. Due to the sepsis, I was still not out of the woods and required various different types of intravenous antibiotics. I was not alert for many days, my legs and feet were extremely swollen and I was on a liquid diet.

The doctors had recommended a machine to be put on my legs and feet to simulate walking to help assist with the swelling since I couldn't walk. I recall being extremely groggy, anxious and incoherently upset and distressed at times, not knowing where I was or what happened to me. Immediately after surgery and being transferred to ICU, I had somehow started bleeding out and required several blood transfusions. One particular day when my mom came by to see me she described being absolutely shocked and traumatised. As she walked into the room, I was still unconscious but suddenly my chest started to constrict heavily as if I were gasping for air. The machines attached to me started to beep ferociously and nurses and doctors came running my way. My mom was ushered out while they worked on me, trying to stabilise me. My mom feared that I had gotten COVID-19 while in hospital. She waited for them to let her in.

The doctors managed to get it under control. 'Mom, she had an asthma attack, likely due to the stress on her body, but we got everything under control now and will have a pulmonary specialist attend to her as well going forward.'

My mom didn't really know what to say; she was still devastated by what she had seen. She asked if she would be able to stay with me for a bit and the doctors said yes but they would be bringing a mobile X-ray machine by to check my lungs shortly.

I woke up feeling groggy and tired, my eyes felt heavy and my abdomen hurt. I was surprised to see my mom sitting there. I felt defeated and fed up with everything I had been through. I didn't want to do any more procedures, I just wanted to be left alone. I felt like so far everything that could go wrong had gone wrong, I looked at my mom and said, 'Mommy, I am tired, I don't want to do this anymore. I am suffering so much; I am so tired and in pain.'

My mom looked at me intensely and said, 'I know, but you have to hold on.'

In my incoherent and exhausted voice, I said, 'I am ready to go, they shouldn't do anything else to resuscitate me, I am ready to die.'

My mom wouldn't accept it.

I started to fall asleep again and felt myself being moved and shifted. I tried to open my heavy eyelids to see what was happening but I couldn't keep them open. I caught a glimpse of a machine moving towards me, which I now know is the mobile X-ray machine.

When I woke up again, my mom was standing at my bedside. She squeezed my hand and said, 'I need to tell you something.'

Somehow I knew what she wanted to tell me and I couldn't hear it then. 'Not now, I can't,' I said.

I later found out that my publisher and friend Nadia Goetham had died due to COVID-19 in a hospital not far from the one I was in, around the same time I was struggling to breathe.

Recovery was incredibly hard and painful. I was covered in pipes and apparatus, including an IV with multiple components. I couldn't bathe myself, and I was being 'fed' through an IV attached to a big bag that looked like it contained milk to make sure I was getting the nutrients I needed. I was still on antibiotics and morphine. My regular IV site in my arm was changed for a more semi-permanent line on my right wrist and right upper chest area. The lines were stitched to keep them in instead of just secured with medical tape; it was painful to move my arm too much. My anxiety and distress became so intense that I had to have a psychiatrist see me daily in ICU to address some of my concerns. I didn't think seeing the psychiatrist would help with my terror, anxiety and fear. He was a nice-enough older man with a head of grey hair but I didn't feel like he understood me, my circumstances or what I was going through. He was quite clinical and tried to get me to focus on 'getting back on the horse' as he liked to say to me. In truth, I felt like I had been on a horse that was bucking and wilding all my life. I didn't want to be on the ride anymore, I didn't want to have to just kap aan, which had been the theme of my life. I just wanted someone to hear my fears and anxiety and to allow me to feel it without instructing me to keep going. I needed softness and understanding more than ever.

Seeing the psychiatrist felt like a daily chore, like I was working to appease him and keep on with the theme of getting back on the horse. I refrained from expressing my real feelings of despair and debilitating stress for fear that I would be pushed to see a silver lining. The psychiatrist would say to me, 'You know, sometimes, it's better to keep going and get back into things to avoid getting too overwhelmed and unable to get back to the things you need to do.' And yes, I mean, fair enough, but I had been in survival mode all my life dealing with things I had no control over. I just didn't have it in me in that moment.

I suppose ICU is a complicated space. It is one where people are often unconscious, not responsive, and in a state of emergency; there was a stark difference in treatment from ICU nurses to other nurses. They often added to my panic by being incredibly harsh and impatient, devoid of any kind of emotional intelligence, unable to empathise with another human. I would often experience my machine alarms blaring because my breathing and heart rate had changed, just for nurses to run my way and scold me for panicking: 'If you stop panicking and breathe normally, the machine will stop,' a nurse would say in an abrupt tone with a scowl that would make anyone shudder. I mean how often have you heard of someone being told to stop panicking and it actually working?

I was afraid that I wouldn't get better, but also afraid that I would need more procedures. I was traumatised by everything that had already happened. I was worried about work and leave because of the extended stay in hospital. I had multiple panic attacks in hospital because of the stress and anxiety. I hated the loudness of ICU, not in the normal sense of the word loud but more so the sound of constant beeping, machines, worse yet running. I dreaded the mornings in ICU – the minute nurses started walking around with their medicine trolleys, I clenched my teeth in anticipation of what was to come. Even nurses felt bad for patients as they administered an injection called Clexane to prevent blood clots particularly in the legs, a necessary drug for immobile patients. It was excruciating – it felt like a form of torture. The needle itself was enormous but the medicine burned so severely that it left a hot red mark and the effects could be felt for weeks after. Each morning nurses would look through notes and try to see where they had administered the drug previously so that they could try somewhere else instead of hurting the same spot. I would hope they would forget but they never did. 'Okay, Miss Dirks, where should we do it today?' they would ask. 'Because, as you know, we can do your thighs or belly, but for you with all your abdominal incisions, we would probably do thighs only.' I contemplated asking them to do it in my belly, since it was already extremely painful and swollen. Besides, my thigh felt numb and like it was persistently burning, so I settled on the left thigh. It felt like I was being impaled each time with a hot ice pick. The nurse would say, 'I am so sorry, just keep still so we can get it over with, okay? Just try to breathe,' as she cleaned the area and got ready to inject the molten lava. I was grateful for the nurses who would offer me an ice pack to hold on the site afterwards. I put it out of my mind as if I would never have to do it again, until the next day.

I realised that trying to get up and walk, one day after a surgery, holding my stapled belly together with a clean towel was less painful than daily Clexane shots. Maybe that's the purpose of it – to force patients to mobilise, and it's a helluva incentive.

My mom had been in touch with the director of the organisation I worked for, who became increasingly difficult, requesting daily updates from my mom, including photos. The director had received direct correspondence from Dr Blaauw, but still hounded my mom – supposedly out of concern.

I yearned to go home so badly; I didn't want to be in hospital anymore. Days had gone by and I was still in ICU due to the surgery, sepsis and all the added complications. A woman named Neo came by and told me she was a physical therapist. 'I am going to assist with physical therapy especially surrounding your lungs. Asthma and laying down for extended periods of time can cause water to accumulate in the lungs. We don't want that.'

It was kind of nice to have someone else to speak to outside of doctors and nurses; I didn't mind because for the first time in weeks I could sit up by myself, unplugged and unattached to a bunch of wires and monitors. For an hour every day Neo would come and unplug me, even from the machine that moved my feet and legs, and sit me up to do my lung physical therapy. She would put a clean towel on my abdominal incision first and then lightly tap my back with a metal machine that vibrated. 'Okay now try and cough for me if you can. I know it can make your abdominal incision hurt so be gentle. Hold the towel to yourself lightly for support.' And I would hold the towel with both hands, palms down and cough a bit to clear my lungs. Sometimes I would cough up phlegm, which Neo would beam about.

'That's great!' she'd exclaim.

Next she would have me blow into a little plastic contraption to move the ball as high as I could, this she said was to strengthen my lungs. Sometimes I would get tired but we needed to do around ten. Neo encouraged me to do the exercise a few times a day if I could.

'Please try throughout the day, I promise it will help you heal so much faster.'

I didn't know how that would work but, honestly, I would try anything to heal and get better soon. I hated the dread I felt. I just wanted to be able to live the life I intended to live but everything felt so uncertain. Every morning, all of my doctors would stop by and check in on me. Each day I would hope they would agree that I could be moved to a regular ward.

One rainy morning, after my doctor's visits, my favourite nurse Khosi came in smiling.

'Guess what?!' she said.

I said, 'What?'

She started to laugh. 'You are leaving ICU today!'

I started to cry out of relief. Surely this meant I was on the mend and soon I would be out of the monochromatic, horribly lit and loud ICU. Khosi came over and hugged me. She started to fill out paperwork to prepare my discharge. She came to my bed and said, 'Okay, I am going to remove the stitches from your wrist and chest lines, ne?'

I said, 'Okay, I don't think it will be as painful as it is while attached to my arm anyway.'

Khosi laughed as she started to clean my wrist area. 'Hold still, ne, sisi,' she said.

She used a scalpel and quickly cut the stitches and gently pulled the line out and then held down with a chunk of cotton wool to stop the bleeding, before adding a dressing and doing the same to the chest line.

I was ecstatic to finally be moved from ICU to a regular ward, it felt like I was getting closer to recovery and eventually being discharged. I was taken from ICU to a relatively full ward with two other women who helped me tremendously. I didn't feel so alone even though my mom needed to get back to Cape Town for work and would only be returning in a few days.

Charnay was a young woman around my age. She was tall and wore glasses. Sherazaan was about ten years my senior. Charnay was in the bed to my left and Sherazaan was across from me. They were warm, we shared snacks and spoke about our lives and suddenly hospital didn't feel so lonely and scary. They were intrigued by my being Capetonian and asked me how life was in Cape Town. They were both from the townships in Johannesburg and told me how common gang violence was. Charnay was discharged within a day, but the evening before was terrifying. Charnay's baby had died inside of her and she had been given medication to essentially abort the foetus. She was in so much pain as the contraction pains intensified. She was left alone with no one checking up on her and she groaned in pain. I tried to look over but her curtains were partially closed. I figured that meant not to disturb her but she sounded terrible.

'Are you okay?' I asked quietly.

'No ... I'm not, I am in so much pain and the sister left and didn't come back. She even left my curtains closed.'

I knew how claustrophobic that could be, especially when you're unable to open them yourself. Sherazaan heard this and, since she was the only one between us without a catheter or other wires inhibiting movement, got up and opened Charnay's curtain for her. She looked at us both and said, 'You know, my baby just stopped moving, I knew something was wrong but I didn't expect this.'

She choked up. We all just lay in our beds, silent for a second, feeling the grief and hurt with her.

'I'm really sorry this is happening to you,' I said.

She smiled faintly, half grimacing through the pain. We stayed up with Charnay all night as she mourned the loss of the baby she wanted. She asked us to call a nurse for her. 'I need pain killers, I can't do this,' she said softly. She lifted the thin sheet covering her up to show us the crimson-soaked bedsheets beneath her – she had been sitting in her own blood unable to call for a nurse.

The following morning, we wished Charnay luck – she was headed to theatre to remove any additional tissue. 'See you both soon,' she said.

'Good luck, sis, sien jou nou nou,' said Sherazaan, sitting in her Pikachu onesie with her hood on.

I laughed at the sight of her and told Charnay, 'It will be fast and you'll be okay, I promise,' I said.

I knew she would be, she had to be. I couldn't accept anything differently.

After about two hours, she was back and groggy. 'How am I?' she asked us.

'Good, you just need to rest, and then they will let you go home tomorrow,' I said.

She smiled as she closed her eyes and drifted off to sleep. I lay my head down on my pillow, teary and envious of Charnay getting to leave the next day. I tried to push aside my feelings as selfish but I just wanted to go home so badly.

Charnay leaving was rough on me. I had less distraction and had to confront my own issues, which I had been conveniently avoiding. At least Sherazaan was still there with me. I was still wearing a catheter which sucked and hurt every time it was too full, or I moved wrong, or needed to get up to go to the bathroom. I could finally bathe myself using the basin and sitting down on a chair. The sense of independence was such an enormous shift from the past weeks. I stood up to change the water in the basin. I looked at myself in the mirror in front of me and didn't recognise myself or my body. I looked haggard – my hair was untidy, my face looked swollen, my naked body looked like someone else's. I had wound dressings all over my abdomen and pelvic region; I looked swollen and discoloured. I had giant stretch marks that looked like tiger markings on the sides of my abdomen. I had the catheter in place and a wound dressing where my intravenous ports were. My arms were blue and yellow, showing various degrees of healing of the places where blood was taken. I just stared, hoping the distorted images would change to something I knew. I scanned my body, looking for something I recognised.

I heard a knocking sound in the distance and then a voice. 'Sisi, are you okay? Do you need me to help you bath?' the nurse asked.

I snapped out of it, sliding back into the chair, staring at the mirror, 'No, sister, I'm okay,' I said shakily.

I tried to finish cleaning myself without looking at the distortion in the mirror. I didn't know that person anyway.

When I finished bathing and came back out to go back to my bed, Sherazaan was sitting on her bed talking to a woman I didn't know. From the conversation I quickly gathered that it was her doctor. Sherazaan looked really happy, 'So, from how things are going, I really think if your blood tests are fine and you feel fine in the morning, then you can go home,' the doctor said to her.

Sherazaan and I made eye contact and she beamed at me. I smiled back, trying to be happy for her too. I was glad she was getting better, I was just dreading being by myself and still not being ready to go home just yet.

The morning came and Sherazaan was packed up and ready to go. Her doctor had given her the go ahead. We shared goodbyes and well wishes before I watched her walk out in her Pikachu onesie. I felt the waves of anxiety come over me like a tsunami. I felt panicked. 'Why has everyone else gotten better and been released but me?' I asked myself. I knew there was no way I was going home since my catheter was still in and I was still on intravenous medication, and that didn't help the mental state I found myself in.

The reality of Nadia's death suddenly dawned on me. I started feeling that lump in my throat threatening to push me to the brink of hysterics. My urologist walked into the now empty ward. He was wearing a white kufiya and a long white thobe.

'Miss Dirks, what's wrong now?' he asked.

His tone made me want to shove a sock in his mouth – what about the situation I was in wasn't inherently wrong? I looked at him, trying to swallow my tears. 'I just want to go home. I don't want to be here, I want this catheter out. I am mourning my friend.'

He looked at me, puzzled; I suppose trying to piece together my list of things making me want to go home. He started with the medical. 'Well, we can't remove the catheter – it isn't a normal catheter and we can't pull at it because there is a risk that it will cause trauma if we try too soon.'

I tried to express the discomfort and pain, which he put down as 'normal'.

I started wailing about Nadia. 'She was supposed to come see me, she didn't come see me, and now she's gone because of COVID,' I said through tears.

He looked through my folder, standing in front of me, and said, 'Well, you know the Almighty works in mysterious ways. Think about it this way: Maybe if she did come and visit you then you would also be dealing with COVID, so maybe it was for the best.'

I must have disassociated because I don't have any memory of responding to him or him leaving but I do recall being stunned at his response – how cold and callous, how minimising to put our entire relationship down to the fact that she had somehow saved me by staying away. I detested the urologist and tried not to speak to him unless absolutely necessary. To me, he was cruel and unfeeling. I guess if asked I would describe him as a medical robot who could only focus on the medical aspects of patients but not the emotional aspects, but I guess, at the same time, he must have been traumatised by all the deaths the healthcare sector had suddenly seen overnight due to the pandemic. I suppose it is a strange form of defence and self-preservation to keep going.

I started to feel better physically and just wanted to go home but my daily blood tests, which monitored signs of infection, were just not lowering fast enough to an acceptable amount, according to my doctors. I tried to convince my surgeon that I was better but he looked at me like I had two heads and said, 'Nadine, your CRP is 489 currently. To put it into perspective for you, a normal CRP rate is under 10. A CRP rate of over 50 is considered to be severe elevation. In general, over 200 is still considered a marker of sepsis. So, while you may be feeling better because you are on intravenous medicines, you are still not healthy enough to go home right now.'

The numbers had me absolutely spiralling.

'Okay, so what now? What happens now?' I asked him.

'Well ... you need to stay here on medication and not stress because stress could hinder your healing.'

The ward was empty. There were four beds and I was in the bed closest to the window. The view seemed so drab because all I could see were the other sides of the hospital. I tried to put on a brave face and rest. I tried to walk around the ward when I had the energy; every day the nurse would take me for a walk around the section I was in to make sure I was mobilising and getting better.

My workplace began to put incredible pressure onto me, as if I wasn't already trying to get better as soon I could. They made me feel as if I went on a month-long vacation in the Bahamas without letting them know. Unfortunately, I couldn't control my health situation. I was flustered trying to figure out solutions and thinking about whether I could try and do some work while in hospital. The director sent me a message saying she hoped I got better soon, and added, 'Especially because I am now having to do a lot of your tasks as well as my work.' It felt like a guilt trip but what was I supposed to do? Go to work in a hospital bed? The constant check-ins started to feel more like hounding than helpful. She demanded updates and explicit details as to my medical condition. My endometriosis specialist found it incredibly frustrating and said 'I have sent her your updated medical note, she has my details, why is she bothering someone in hospital for details? Besides, you don't need to disclose anything to her.' He instructed me to ignore her messages and to focus on my healing, and I did. As my CRP levels continued to drop, I was finally discharged from hospital but I had a stent in my left ureter, which had to be removed.

A few days into my recovery at home, the director called me again. She had a long-winded way of speaking that would keep me on the phone for 45 minutes to an hour; it absolutely drained me.

'You know, Nadine,' she started to say, 'I was talking to a therapist who works with our organisation about your medical situation and experience and she has said that she thinks you will need professional medical assistance in terms of a psychiatrist and a therapist.'

'Yes, I know, I have been seeing both,' I said, hoping to stop the conversation and get off the phone as soon as possible.

'Good, well, what she was saying is that you are likely unfit to work for a while because of everything that happened and how traumatic it was.'

I tried not to sound as irritated as I felt – why was she discussing intimate details of my health and trauma with a person I had never met, against my consent? What was the point of this and why did they think they could speak on my behalf regarding what I can and cannot do? I felt like my privacy had been violated on so many levels and she didn't seem to see the fault in what she had done.

'I am sure with intensive therapy and taking things one day at a time that I will be okay,' I said.

She interjected and said, 'Oh, so if you are seeing a psychiatrist and therapist could you ask them to send me a report regarding what you two have discussed and their findings so I can see where you are at?'

I was blown away. I paused, unsure how to answer her. Surely, she couldn't be serious? Why would my employer need such personal details?

'I will discuss it with them,' I said.

I couldn't figure her out; nor could I figure out her intentions. She wasn't exactly helpful but she definitely felt exceptionally nosy. I was worried about my job purely because her behaviour was alarming.

My endometriosis specialist asked me to visit his outpatient consulting rooms for a check-up a few days after my discharge. My mom accompanied me to the appointment. A friendly woman sat behind the desk and let us in.

'Doctor will be with you soon. Would you like any tea or coffee?' she asked us.

My mom looked at me to see if I wanted any, I shook my head no.

'No, thank you, we're okay,' my mom said as my doctor came out to call us to his office.

Mom had many questions for him. She wanted to know what went wrong and she wanted to know if I would be okay.

'How do you feel?' he asked me, but he looked at my mom instead. I suppose he didn't want me just saying 'I'm fine' out of fear of hospitalisation. My mom looked at me, searching my face, before saying, 'She's okay, but she has lots of pain and discomfort, and she's very traumatised by the whole situation; it has been so complicated and unbelievable how everything has gone wrong.'

I intentionally disassociated, focusing on the row of trees outside the doctor's office, the wind threatening to knock them down like dominoes. I stopped listening to what my mom was saying. I was catapulted back into reality when Dr Blaauw started to speak in his thick Dutch accent. 'I understand, Mrs Dirks,' he said to my mom. 'To be honest, in all my years treating and operating on patients with endometriosis, Nadine has the worst, most severe and aggressive form of endometriosis I have ever seen.'

I sat there emotionless, looking down at my Crocs, pretending they were talking about someone else and not me. Acknowledging that they were talking about me and how severe my endometriosis was would likely have caused a nervous breakdown. I couldn't stop to break down and feel the severity of his words; it just wouldn't leave me in a space where I could still manage to keep going.

My mom asked, 'Will she be okay?'

Dr Blaauw paused. 'Well, yes, but she will never not have severe endometriosis and that is the challenge,' he answered.

He got up and asked us to follow him to another room with a hospital bed. 'Could you help her undress and put on a gown please, Mrs Dirks?'

My mom grabbed my arm to help me get to the other side of the room. Behind the big blue screen, we found a clean folded hospital gown and a basket for used ones. Mom helped me change so Dr Blaauw could examine me and remove the staples from the incisions in my belly. As he tugged on each individual staple, he continued to talk – I suspect to keep me calm.

'You are still quite swollen but it's okay, it's nothing to be too concerned about, you seem to be healing really well otherwise.'

I was glad, I just wanted to put this portion of my life in a box and throw away the key. My mom stood at my feet, watching the doctor remove the staples. She smiled at me and mouthed, 'Almost done!' I smiled back at her, grateful that she could be there with me.

I saw a psychiatrist, named Dr Naidoo, a few days later who worked in a clinic close to where I lived. She was a dark-haired woman with a beautiful office. My therapist had already forwarded her some insights into my experience, so she was well aware. She asked me to sit down on the brown leather chair in front of her desk and asked me, 'How are you?'

The question and the sincerity with which she asked the question turned me into a bawling mess, unable to string a sentence together. I just sobbed. 'It's okay, cry, it's okay,' she said as she handed me some tissues.

I tried to compose myself and answer her. 'I am not okay… I am worried about work, I feel alone and I feel like I just can't catch a break with my health. Everything that could go wrong has gone wrong and I feel defeated,' I said.

She nodded and I continued. 'The director of the company I work for has spoken to a therapist I don't know and have never spoken to, who has now said I have experienced trauma and so I may not be fit to work. She has also asked for notes from my therapist and psychiatrist to see where I am at mentally.'

The psychiatrist's face changed from empathetic and soft to protective and annoyed. 'I don't see why she needs access to your personal medical information unless you want her to have it. Do you?' she asked. I sat and looked up at the beautiful abstract art above my psychiatrist's head and thought about it. I looked back at her and said, 'No, I don't, but I feel like she is forceful and I don't know how to get her off my back.' Doctor Naidoo nodded and said, 'Well, then, that's that. She has no right to see them.' Before I could say anything, she asked me, 'Do you feel suicidal? Do you feel like you want to hurt yourself?'

The question sent me into a state again. I hyperventilated trying to speak through tears. Doctor Naidoo gently handed me more tissues and said, 'Take a deep breath in and out, just cry, it's okay, you don't have to speak if you can't right now.'

I breathed in and out a few times and cried into the palms of my hands. Her question struck a nerve for me. I wasn't suicidal in the traditional sense of the word, and I also had no intention of harming myself, but I was so tired of the trauma associated with my health. I explained, 'I am tired of having to do so many procedures, hospital stays and dealing with the aftermath of that over and over again. I am not suicidal but at times I do feel like this is never ending and that I have suffered and my body and mind are just not able to keep up anymore.'

She nodded and smiled and said, 'I hear you and understand, I am so sorry that this is happening to you.'

Doctor Naidoo asked me, 'How do you feel about being booked in as an inpatient for a while so you can rest and recover here with in-person mental healthcare support? Or do you prefer to do outpatient care?' The thought of being admitted to a hospital again made my skin crawl, I just couldn't do it again. I just wanted to be at home, in my own space. I wanted to be at home in Cape Town even more. I felt that being with my family and in a familiar space would be good for me. Doctor Naidoo agreed, 'Could you send an email to your manager and the director and request that once you are cleared medically that you go to Cape Town and work from there since you are working remotely anyway due to the pandemic?'

It sounded like a good idea. I didn't have to be in office, so why not? I went home and sent the email just as we had discussed. Within minutes I got an email back from the director. I opened it up nervously. 'Nadine,' she wrote. 'This is a request that I would have to discuss with our board members, while we work remotely currently we do expect all employees to be in Gauteng, and besides we can't let one person leave because then everyone will request to go back home to see their families.'

The urge to reply and say 'It is not the same fucking thing as just wanting to go home to see my family' was strong but I tried to be professional, hoping the board members would be way more reasonable, so I let it go. A few days had gone by before I got an email back from the director letting me know that the board members had declined my request. I was relatively unsurprised at that point until I got to the next paragraph wherein she demanded that by the end of the month 'I expect to see you back at work.'

I panicked because I knew it just wouldn't be possible. I still had a stent that needed to be removed, which would require a day or two in hospital if everything goes well. I felt cornered. So much for being passionate about reasonable accommodation and, since they were a mental healthcare organisation, I would expect them to be more considerate.

Being home largely by myself was difficult. My mom and sister had to get back to Cape Town and I was left with wandering thoughts and debilitating anxiety. I was finally able to access my emails. I wasn't nearly ready for weeks of unattended emails, particularly from my medical aid and the hospital I was in. It ping ponged from costs from the hospital per incident to emails from my medical aid saying they couldn't pay for some parts of my care or that they would only pay a portion of the amount. I sat in my living room, on my dark blue couch, feeling like I couldn't get enough air into my lungs. 'How am I ever going to pay this off?' I thought, while looking at the amounts R38 000 for the anaesthesiologist, R59 450 for the endometriosis specialist, R9 230 for the blood bank, R20 000 for scans, R11 750 for the psychiatrist, R34 767 for physical therapy. I stopped reading when I realised these costs were just for the first surgery and I had not even gotten to the second surgery. I felt dread wash all over my body, paralysing me as I tried to move. I took deep breaths in and out a few times before exploding into painful, snotty ugly tears. I was in a bind for the rest of my life, and there was no one to turn to. I didn't come from money and I couldn't depend on my working-class family to get me out of this. The emails said I needed to pay these bills within 30 days. I had been in hospital for so long that these were way overdue. I decided to email the service providers and be honest about what was going on at least. Even if they were overdue, I figured at least I would try to get in touch and possibly make arrangements to pay it off. I let them know I had been hospitalised again and had an additional surgery and that I was on unpaid leave and unable to make payments immediately. I would be in touch as soon as I felt better regarding a potential payment plan. Nearly all got back to me on the same day saying a variation of the same thing: 'We are sorry to hear about the additional surgery, we hope you get well soon, thank you for letting us know, we are happy to do a payment plan once you are back on your feet.' I sighed in relief. I just didn't know how else to manage the situation since it felt as if my work circumstances were falling apart.

During my recovery at home my sister had noticed that I whimpered in my sleep, sometimes sobbing, but I had no recollection in the morning. I was certain it would let up but it only worsened. I started to experience awful nightmares every night often with a similar theme: I was stuck in a hospital bed somewhere outside in a hallway that resembled a school of some kind. I would be conscious but unable to move, get up, or even scream for help. When people walked past me it seemed like they couldn't see me and wouldn't stop to help me even though I tried to reach out in distress but my wrists and ankles were shackled to the bed. I woke up with my heart beating out of my chest, drenched in a cold sweat, with a pillow wet with my tears. It felt so real that, when I woke up, I would look around my bedroom in a state of terror, trying to identify where I was before trying to lift my arm to check if my wrists were still bound. I always made sure to make a note for my therapist on my phone – she encouraged me to try a technique called a body scan when I felt anxious and in pain; she would say, 'It may help you reduce chronic pain by acknowledging the pain and focusing on where you feel it and it could also be beneficial for your anxiety and sleep so you don't feel so out of control.'

I had felt so disempowered and out of control that while being still and trying to slowly scan through my body, engaging with the things that happened to me, I would often try and put it out of my mind in order to cope because I didn't think I could manage facing it head on. I think in some ways it helped me not only process the things that happened but also helped me gently face the trauma at my own pace. We also spoke often about my workplace woes and ways to engage with the director that were on my terms and didn't leave me in a crisis. I tried to ensure that I didn't take unsolicited calls during my recovery time and instead communicated via email and through scheduled calls. This way I could anticipate the call and prepare myself for some of what the director would say to me. I scheduled a call for after a nap and the director called to check on me. Every conversation with her felt like a game of cat and mouse. After exchanging pleasantries, she said, 'You know, it's for the best that you aren't going back home because surely you will just be lying at home by yourself while your parents are at work.'

I didn't really get her point or why she felt the need to say that, since we had already established that they would not allow me to go home to recover, so her bringing it up again just felt like a way to mess with me. I tried to change the subject and said, 'I am dedicated to my job and I love it, I'm just so heartbroken that all these things have happened with me and my health right now.'

Her tone shifted from playing nice to snarky. 'Well,' she said, 'we took a chance on you and I guess it didn't pay off.'

I was blown away, I felt a sharp ache in my stomach, what was she trying to say to me? How was it taking a chance on me? I was brilliant at my job; I was more than qualified, educated and I had extensive experience. The entire comment felt like a microaggression – what chance did they have to take on me? I am not a betting horse, I thought. I tried to get off the phone as soon as I could, I didn't want to end up asking her what the hell she meant. I decided to keep my head down – after all, I really needed the job given the mountains of medical debt and I did love my job and Johannesburg. I needed to focus on resting and healing so I could get back into the swing of things at work.

This tief is trying to take me out

I NOTICED THAT I HAD some stomach discomfort and constipation a few days before my check-up with Dr Blaauw. At my appointment, I made sure to let him know. He sat in his chair with his hands folded as I spoke.

'Okay, so, it could be that you have some loops of bowel causing an issue but I think it is unlikely since your surgery was a while ago. For now, I will give you a prescription and we will watch the constipation.'

I said okay, pleased with his response that it was most likely nothing serious that required additional surgery.

He wrote the prescription down and handed it to me, saying 'Just watch out for a fever, nausea, and just feeling in pain – if anything is out of the ordinary, let me know, okay?' He asked me to be in touch. I felt hopeful for the first time in a while – it seemed the dust had settled and I was finally on the mend. I felt at ease about going back to work in about a week and started planning what I would do for the week leading up to going back to work. I was in a good space regarding work and felt that there was no way the director could be difficult since I would be back soon.

But the stomach pain seemed to worsen – it felt like it was in the pit of my stomach. I wondered if perhaps due to all the stress I had been going through I could possibly be developing a stomach ulcer. I tried to not take my pain medication on an empty stomach, and got some over-the-counter medication for ulcers and heartburn, and something for stomach cramps. I didn't think too much of it and just put it down to stress. I figured that the constipation could be due to endometriosis and because of the pain medication. I drank the sickly-sweet thick syrup my doctor prescribed to help me deal with the constipation. It still didn't seem to be working as effectively as it had before. The pain started to worsen but it didn't seem intense enough to warrant going back to the hospital. I just assumed I needed to rest and take it easy.

I was scheduled to finally remove the stent from my ureter into my kidney during the third wave of COVID-19, which saw hospitals unable to contain the fallout. My urologist suggested that we remove the stent in his office instead of admitting me to hospital and taking me to theatre to remove the stent. I was nervous since I already had multiple issues due to the stent causing spasms and kidney infections but I figured it may be my safest option given that being admitted to hospital seemed to carry a grave risk of contracting COVID-19.

The urologist said, 'It is an easy and quick procedure. We use a thin tube with a small camera that is able to grab onto the stent and then we pull it out.'

It sounded horrible to me but I didn't want to get admitted again so I bit down and agreed. Jamil agreed to drive me in the pouring rain to my morning appointment. He accompanied me inside to a large waiting room with comfortable plush orange chairs and various rakkams on the wall. The waiting room was empty aside from a woman in a blue uniform mopping an area in vain as the rain kept seeping through a leak in the ceiling. The receptionist was a nors woman with a permanent scowl. She didn't greet and barked orders: 'Sit down! Doctor will be with you when he is ready.'

We sat down and waited. I was nervous and didn't know what to expect; my stomach ached severely and I just wanted to know how long it would take. Eventually the urologist rounded the corner with a smile and said, 'Nadine, you can come through.'

I looked at Jamil and got up to follow the doctor. His office had lots of dark wood. He took a seat behind his dark mahogany desk and I took a seat opposite him.

'How are you doing, Nadine?' he asked.

I sat there with the worst stomach pain I had felt in a while but thought it had no bearing on the reason I was there to see the urologist. By the time I saw him I had already been severely constipated and using multiple types of laxatives to attempt to alleviate the constipation and stomach pain.

'I am okay, just nervous, thanks for asking,' I answered meekly.

'Okay, so, today, we are going to remove your stent, as you know. First I am going to clean the area, and then put some medications into a catheter to help numb the area. Once we do that, I will insert a very thin tube with a camera so I can watch everything on the monitor before using the same tube to grip the stent and gently pull it out. It should be a fairly quick and easy procedure.'

I nodded, grateful that it didn't sound too complicated.

'There is a gown in the room behind you. Please change and lie down on the bed. I will be in in a few minutes and we will begin, okay?'

I nodded again and walked to the room behind me. It was small and almost seemed sterile, all white, with just a few drawers of medical apparatus, the bed, a chair and a monitor above the foot end of the bed. I quickly changed, putting my clothes on the little bench. I put the gown on and lay down on the bed with my hands interlocking on my chest nervously.

The urologist knocked and came in. He washed his hands thoroughly, dried them and put on a new pair of gloves from the metal cart next to the bed. 'I am going to tell you when to take a deep breath and exhale, okay?'

'Okay,' I said.

He asked me to spread my legs before using a cold wet piece of gauze to clean the urethra. I looked up at the ceiling, afraid that if I looked at what he was doing, that I would freak out and panic.

'Breathe in,' he said and I did.

I felt a sharp pain for a second, and cold wetness.

'That's good, you are doing well,' he said. He looked at the monitor while working and told me to breathe in deeply and exhale again. I felt discomfort and slight pain before he announced, 'There you go, all done!' holding a thin flexible tube.

I was puzzled, I expected it to be way worse and I assumed it would take a while.

'Are we done?' I asked in disbelief.

'Yes, we are,' he said as he wiped the area with saline water and gauze once again. 'You can get up and get dressed. There are some paper towels next to you if you need them,' he said, taking off his gloves, heading out the door.

'Thank you,' I said.

I got up and grabbed the paper towel to soak up the saline water which had made its way to my back and thighs. I removed the drenched hospital gown, put it in a plastic laundry basket and got dressed. I thought maybe the stomach pain would subside now, given that I had one less thing to stress about.

Jamil was surprised to see me back in the waiting room so fast.

'You're done?' he asked in disbelief.

'Yup!' I answered in excitement.

When I got home, I nervously went to the bathroom, knowing that the first urination would probably feel like a lake of fire; my stomach ached more than usual. I thought maybe I needed some stronger medication that would help with an ulcer.

Jamil suggested we take a drive to Hartbeespoort Dam on Sunday and I couldn't wait! I was counting down the days before our drive. It was only three days but I hadn't done anything normal in a while. In the meantime, I spent the rest of my weekend trying to prepare for work in the coming week, getting enough rest and watching *Living Single*. My stomach pain worsened; I felt nauseous and had no appetite. I convinced myself it was because I was anxious about going back to work again. I tried eating dry Salticrax and brought the box to my bed amongst other things I needed and didn't have the energy to get up and fetch each time I needed them. My stomach protested, punching and kicking me internally.

I thought maybe eating some crackers would help but it didn't; eventually I settled on a combination of two Panados, one Buscopan and one omeprazole. It seemed to keep the situation under control enough for me to watch my show and fall asleep.

On Saturday I opened my eyes but the sun streaming into my small bedroom seemed off. It wasn't as bright or low. I grabbed my phone and realised I had yet again slept the day away – but I still felt exhausted. I sent Jamil a message letting him know I didn't think I could do a drive to Harties because I wasn't feeling well. My appetite was strange, I felt weak, I was still constipated and the pain in my stomach worsened. I noticed that when I breathed in too deeply, I experienced a sharp pain in the chest. I didn't really worry about it and assumed it was because of the uncomfortable position I was lying in at the time. For the rest of Saturday, I tried to eat and hydrate as much as I could – I had to get better and get over this hurdle. I was expected to be at work bright eyed and bushy tailed on Monday.

I passed out in the early evening and woke to intensive stabbing pain and weakness; something was wrong.

I panicked, uncertain about what to do next. I decided to call my mom. She answered swiftly, 'Hello, how are you? How are you feeling?' she asked me. The minute I heard her voice I started to sob – it was as if it dawned on me that I was not well at all, it was a moment of clarity for me. I had to face the facts. I told my mom I felt sick and she asked how.

'I don't know, I just feel exhausted, drowsy, and in a lot of pain. I can't eat anything and I've been constipated for over a week,' I said.

A part of me was hoping for some sage mom advice, like to drink some hot water and lemon; instead, she jumped into action. She listened attentively and said hang on before hanging up. She called me back and said, 'I called your doctor and he said he is still in his rooms at the hospital and he will wait for you to get there. I called Jamil and he is also on his way to take you there.'

In the meantime, I decided to pack my hospital bag just in case I was ordered to be admitted. Jamil arrived in 10 minutes. He didn't ask me any intense questions or require me to explain why I didn't say things were bad, he just silently took my bag from me, put it in the boot of his car and off we went. When we got to the hospital it seemed quiet. Dr Blaauw came out to meet us at the door – his secretary had already gone home and he had no patients. Jamil waited in the waiting area and I went into the office with Dr Blaauw. I sat down as he observed me.

'How are you, your mom said you're unwell?'

'Yes, I don't know what's going on, my stomach hurts, I can't eat and feel nauseous, I keep passing out and sleeping for hours,' I explained.

Dr Blaauw looked down and made notes as we spoke. He looked up at me and said, 'You look fine to me. You can walk and explain what's wrong. It doesn't sound too bad.'

My heart leapt in joy. 'So, I can go home, right?' I said, smiling.

He looked at me almost with a sense of pity and said, 'No, Nadine, no, too much has gone wrong to just let you go, we have to keep you here and monitor you for a few days just in case.'

My mind wandered. I was worried about my family in Cape Town and how this would affect them; I was afraid of how this would affect my work and, honestly, I just didn't want to be admitted to a hospital again. Dr Blaauw said I would need a COVID-19 test so that I could be admitted to a ward. He got up from his desk with his notes in hand and said, 'Let's go, I will walk you guys over to the hospital, okay?'

I walked out to Jamil and asked him to grab my bag from the car as Dr Blaauw locked his offices. Jamil's face dropped. It was quite a chilly day in Johannesburg and the trees all around us seemed to be swaying fiercely in the wind. I said my goodbyes to Jamil so I could get tested and booked in. I sat and waited in pain, hoping that this would just be a formality and that nothing was wrong. My body felt cold when I realised I had to let my workplace know I had been admitted again. I didn't have the energy to hear what the wicked witch of the north of Johannesburg had to say. I called my mom to explain that I would be admitted. She sounded wary about my being admitted.

'Don't worry, I will deal with her,' Mom said regarding the director. 'This is not in your control, so don't worry about her, you just focus on getting better.'

I nodded as if she could see me.

Not this shit again!

I SAT IN THE WAITING ROOM AT the hospital by myself. There were a few others waiting – most seemed to be watching soccer on the TVs in the waiting room. I sat in the front row, eager to get tested for COVID-19 so I could be sent to a ward. My body ached and the metal benches made for an uncomfortable seat. I was called from section to section by nurses who all seemed to be frustrated. Eventually after the paperwork had been filled out and my COVID-19 test came back negative. The nurse called a porter to fetch me in a wheelchair and take me to the ward I was allocated.

When I got to the ward, I realised it was the same section I had been in before. It had five beds, but only two were occupied. I was taken to the very end of the ward near the window, facing a younger woman. The other woman at the other end of the room didn't seem to be awake. I tried to settle in and put my things away. I contemplated taking a shower in case I had to be examined, since taking a shower by myself for the past few days had been nearly impossible. I sat down on my bed to catch my breath first. The woman across from me had left. Next to her bed she had cards and balloons celebrating a baby. I smiled. Soon she returned. She was exceptionally talkative and a little bit too inquisitive for my liking. She came back and introduced herself: 'Hi! I'm Melissa, what's your name?' she said with a bright smile, as she made her way to sit in the seat next to my bed.

I felt sick and uneasy but too unwell to be firm with her, so I told her my name. Melissa harped on and on about her life, her abusive husband and her children for at least an hour before nurses came and told me they needed to insert an intravenous drip. I was relieved, hopefully now she would get the hint and move back to her bed, I needed rest.

'Can I please take a quick shower before the drip, sister?' I asked.

Before the nurse could answer, Melissa piped up: 'Of course, Sr Deirdre is very cool.'

I looked at the nurse for an answer and she said, 'Of course, let me get you a few things and I will be in to help you.'

I was grateful she would assist because Melissa seemed like someone who would follow someone to the bathroom to keep the conversation going. I took out some clean underwear, my toiletry bag and warm pyjamas from my bag as I waited for the nurse. A man walked by in a hospital gown, incoherent and talking to himself; he seemed to be shackled. I couldn't make out what he was saying but he seemed to be looking for someone and hitting himself in the face. I was terrified by him. Thankfully he was in a different room but happened to be in the same ward.

When Sr Deirdre came back I asked, 'Is that man okay? Is he dangerous? He screams and hits himself, it made me bang,' I said.

She smiled and said, 'Don't worry about Wallace. He isn't dangerous at all. He had a severe head injury and he is looking for his wife.'

'I am sorry to hear that,' I said.

Sr Deirdre had a stack of towels and asked me if I was ready to go shower. I followed her to a spacious bathroom with a large shower with mobility aids and a large basin, an additional toilet, and a chair.

'Before we shower, can you please give me a urine sample?' she held out the little cup towards me.

'Yes, okay,' I said.

'Okay, I will give you a few minutes.'

I struggled to balance myself over the small container. I seemed to have gotten some in the container – it wasn't much but it would have to do.

Sr Deirdre knocked at the door. 'Can I come in?' she asked.

'Yes, I am finished,' I answered.

When she walked in I handed her the container. 'I'm sorry sister, I couldn't fill the whole jar.' I motioned to the half empty jar.

'It's okay, don't worry, it's enough,' she smiled.

Sr Deirdre put the towels and my belongings on the chair. She turned on the shower, putting her hand through the water periodically to feel if it were warm enough.

'Can you undress yourself or do you need help?' she asked.

I had already started to undress but needed her help lifting my sweater over my head. Sr Deirdre helped me into the shower. 'Is the water temperature okay?'

'Yes, Sister,' I said.

She helped me wash the areas I couldn't reach and held my hand to balance me so I could wash the areas I could reach.

'Daar soe,' she said as she wrapped a towel around me. She had shifted the clothing to the basin area and helped me get into my warm pyjamas.

'Is there anything else you need?' she asked as she grabbed the used towels and put them in the laundry bin.

'No thank you, just some help to get to my bed please,' I replied.

She took my belongings under her arm and hooked me in with the other, walking slowly across the grey floor. Sr Deirdre put all my belongings away and I got into the bed, making myself comfortable. She gathered the tools and medications for my drip, while Melissa came over to sit next to my bed once again.

Sr Deirdre must have sensed my discomfort and politely said, 'Melissa, you need to get some rest. Jy kannie so op en af wees nie, en die pasient moet ook privacy kry.'

Melissa silently rose and went back to her bed, still staring over at us.

'Okay, so, for now, we are going to give you a normal saline drip because you haven't been eating and drinking. We are also going to send the urine to the lab so they can test and see if anything is wrong. And they are also going to come take a blood sample from you,' she said as she worked on inserting my IV.

'So, for now, it's just monitoring?'

'Yes, we have to monitor you and figure out what's wrong, okay… All done,' she said as the drip seemed to be working effectively.

It was quite cold so I used my big fluffy pink gown as an additional blanket. Melissa noticed and took it as an opportunity to talk to me again.

'It's cold hey? That's why I sleep with my onesie on.' I smiled and agreed it was cold; I was in no mood for small talk. Melissa then asked if I had seen her balloons and cards.

'Yes, congratulations,' I said.

'Well, my husband didn't even get them for me, I got them for myself.'

I didn't really know how to answer her.

'Do you know that my baby died?'

It then dawned on me that she had lost her baby and kept the pink balloons saying 'it's a girl' and congratulatory cards.

'I am so sorry, I don't know what to say, what a horrible thing to happen to anyone.'

Melissa looked at me with hurt all over her face and said, 'It happened last year, I am still not over it and I take my balloons and cards everywhere.'

I was stunned; I thought it was recent. It was clearly an unresolved issue and I guess she just yearned for someone to talk to, someone who would see the balloons and cards and see her and her hurt in a way she needed. Melissa just wanted her pain acknowledged.

I chatted with her for a bit and the staff came around with tea, coffee and biscuits. Melissa asked for milk tea and biscuits, while I asked for some plain rooibos tea. My hands were so cold that my nails started to turn blue. I held onto the hot tea hoping it would warm my cold body. I rang for a nurse, hoping to get another blanket. A different nurse showed up. She was younger, with her hair in a coifed afro.

'Did you ring? What's wrong?' she asked.

'I am cold,' I said, as I stuck my hand out to her to show her my blue nail beds. 'Can I please have another blanket?'

She looked at me with worry. She looked down and counted the layers of blankets and the gown I had on me. 'Just give me a second, I want to get a more senior nurse,' she said.

I rolled my eyes as she walked away. I thought to myself, does she really need a senior nurse's permission to give me another blanket? I lay in the bed shivering, waiting for the nurses to return. The nurse with the afro returned with Sr Deirdre and a cart holding a blood pressure monitor and a thermometer. Sr Deirdre spoke first.

'Nadine, Sr Vuyo said that you are shivering cold, but you have multiple layers on and seem to be the only one getting cold. We think you may have a fever so we want to check that and your vitals first, okay?'

I nodded and said, 'Sure.'

Sr Deirdre looked at the results from the thermometer and said, 'Hai ha uh,' and sister Vuyo tapped her to show her my blood pressure.

'That's too low,' Sr Deirdre said. 'Can you go get her a duvet to make her comfortable?' she instructed as she made notes in a hurry and went to call my doctors.

Sr Deirdre hurried back with another medicine cart; she worked fast adding an entire bottle of medication to the drip. 'This will bring down your fever and help with some of the pain.'

I looked up at the bottle suspended in the air. 'Okay,' I muttered.

Sr Deirdre sat down in the chair next to me. 'So, I spoke with your doctor who admitted you. He advised we give you something for the fever, but he also asked us to book you for a chest X-ray and a CT scan in addition to the blood tests and urine tests.'

I looked at her, studying her face as she spoke.

'Okay, that's fine, when?' I queried.

She looked me in the eye and said, 'Tonight still. There is a list so we have to be patient. If you are asleep, we will wake you up, okay?'

I nodded with a lump in my throat, trying not to cry. Just as Sr Deirdre got up from the chair, a young woman with a little cooler bag walked in towards me. Sr Deirdre motioned to her to come my way. They chatted as Sr Deirdre briefed her on what was needed according to the doctor.

The phlebotomist introduced herself: 'My name is Siphokazi, I am going to take your bloods. Do you have an arm you would prefer I try first?'

I extended my left arm, which was closest to where she was standing; it didn't matter to me anyway. I was crushed. I couldn't believe this could be happening again. It felt so surreal, like one of the nightmares I had been having. When Siphokazi and Sr Deirdre left, I broke down. I tried to cry silently but I just fell apart and sobbed from the depths of my soul. Why was this happening to me? It felt so sinister. Melissa heard me sob and came over to sit in the chair next to my bed again. This time she didn't have much to say, but just rubbed my back and told me, 'I'm sorry, cry it out, it's okay to cry.'

It felt like I needed the permission to just let it all out. I cried until my tears dried up; I couldn't believe this was the hand I had been dealt, again.

The way my luck was set up, my phone rang. I looked down and saw that it was my director calling me. It was 8:30 on a Sunday evening and I was hospitalised. 'Who calls someone in that situation?!' I thought to myself. I decided to answer the phone because I knew my mom had already spoken to her and that she would just end up sending me a series of unpleasant WhatsApp messages.

'Hello, Nadine. How are you?' she asked in an unfriendly, almost suspicious tone.

'I'm okay as can be, I am in hospital again, feeling unwell, how are you?' I responded.

She seemed to be beating about the bush talking about random issues like the fact that she was currently sitting in loadshedding. I looked down at my phone and realised we were already 15 minutes into the call. Suddenly she said, 'I am really worried about the fact that you've chosen to go to hospital knowing you need to be back at work tomorrow.'

I tried to interject and explain that I had no choice in the matter since I was not voluntarily admitted and I was very ill but she continued to speak over me. 'Well, Nadine, I have been forced to do your work while you've been absent and it's taking its toll.'

I tried to apologise and express that it was not my intention to create additional work for her. She continued. 'Nadine, you have to make up your mind as to whether you still want this job because we need a body in this role.' I was blown away by what she said to me and the language used. What kind of a mental healthcare organisation director would call someone and stress their employee out on their hospital bed? Her language was interesting to me since I had chosen to work in non-profit organisations to escape some bits of capitalism but here I was in a situation where yet again I was just a number, just a 'body' in a role that needed to make the machine work smoothly. Her call went on for 45 minutes, leaving me in tears, shaking and hyperventilating. I was conflicted, going back to work or taking care of my health. In many ways I dreaded the director more than I dreaded hospitals and that says a lot.

The porter arrived to take me to get my CT scan done and it felt like a God-given solace – finally I could get off the phone with Cruella. Although I had had a CT scan before, I suddenly felt nervous; it had never really made me feel that way before. The porter and the CT technician helped to move me from my hospital bed onto the thin table-like bed. The machine looked like a giant dome and made me uneasy. I also felt jittery being in a room, vulnerable and alone with a man. I just wanted to get it over with.

The technician explained, 'I will set everything up, and then I will go behind the glass and communicate with you via a microphone, okay?'

'Okay,' I said in a monotone since I had already been through this. He put a different medication into my drip and asked me to lift my arms above my head, which I did. Suddenly I felt a strange warmth radiating throughout my body. I felt as if I needed to urinate, and I could even taste a strange chemical taste in my mouth.

'Is it normal to feel so warm and strange?' I asked. I suspect each time before I wasn't conscious enough to notice.

'Yes, it is, ma'am, it is the iodine, which helps us by changing the colours of your insides so we can see what's wrong,' the technician explained.

He left the room and went behind the glass, giving commands. 'Breathe in for me, okay, now release slowly.'

This went on for what felt like forever. 'Don't worry, we're nearly done,' he let me know.

I was relieved. My stomach hurt and I just wanted to go back to my bed and rest. The technician soon came out from behind the glass. 'The porter will now take you to the X-ray department,' he announced.

'Wait, why? No one said anything about any X-rays, just a CT scan, why?' I protested, not remembering what Sr Diedre had told me. I didn't have the energy to be contorted like some sort of gymnast for an X-ray.

'It's not my choice, just that we have to rule out everything possible. I'm sorry, I can imagine you're in pain.'

The hospital seemed like a ghost town. All the receptionists had gone home; there were no outpatients or visiting relatives, and there were even fewer staff members; it was eerie. On the plus side, at least there were no waiting times and I could be seen shortly. The porter pushed my bed to where the X-ray department was and put my paperwork at my feet.

'She will be with you soon, then I will come back and take you to your ward, mama.'

I smiled at him and said, 'Thank you, ntate.'

The X-ray technician was a young, skinny woman. She wore glasses and her hair in a bun. She opened the door with a smile and walked towards me to push my bed while saying, 'Hi Nadine, my name is Taryn, and I'll be doing your X-rays today.'

She looked at my folder carefully and asked, 'Do you have any jewellery, a bra, or anything like that on you?'

I shook my head no.

Taryn worked fast. 'I don't want to rush this but I also want this to go as smoothly as possible so you can get back to your rest.'

She asked me to stand up in front of an A4-sized medical apparatus, which she lowered to suit my height. She also disappeared behind a glass screen. She kept saying, 'Perfect, just keep still and rest your arms on the machine.'

Before I knew it, it was over. Taryn called the porter and while we waited she helped me get back into my bed and wished me the best of luck.

I looked at her and asked, 'Taryn, is there any way you could tell me if anything was wrong?'

She looked conflicted and said, 'I wish I could, but only the doctors are able to interpret and give results to patients, I'm sorry.'

I understood and wouldn't want her to jeopardise her career. 'That's okay, I am sure they will tell me in the morning.'

The following morning, I woke up and felt much worse. I was in severe pain, and felt drowsy and nauseous.

I noticed that another patient had been admitted – she looked around 18 years old. She kept staring in my direction with a look of fear. I guess seeing another young person in the hospital looking so ill must have been frightening for her even though she just needed her wisdom teeth extracted. I rang for the nurse but they were so busy because of shift changes that it took some time for them to make their way to me. Eventually someone came and I told her how unwell I was feeling and that I needed something I could throw up in because I knew I wouldn't make it to the bathroom on time. I hadn't really eaten for days so I wondered if that was why I was so nauseous or if it was a bug. Since I had hardly eaten, I wondered what my body could possibly eject. The nurse came back with a few disposable kidney-shaped bowls just in case. She put them next to my bed, alongside a glass of ice cubes to help with my nausea. I felt that feeling of my mouth suddenly watering – I knew it was a warning that I was about to throw up. The new girl was still staring at me and for her sake I wished she would stop watching me throw up. I used the remote of the hospital bed to move myself more into a sitting position in case I did throw up. The mouth watering intensified. I quickly grabbed a bowl and threw up with such force that it splattered. It was like nothing I had ever seen before – there were no remnants of food, or anything recognisable. It was a dark green colour, with a thick consistency and the taste was so vile. It was the epitome of the words 'gall bitter'.

I was freaked out, and called for the nurse hysterically. I didn't know what was going on and I was genuinely afraid. The nurse walked in and asked, 'What's wrong?' in a frustrated tone. I showed her the bowl of green sludge. Her eyes widened in shock before she composed herself and called another nurse to come and see.

'It is quite a lot of vomit considering she hasn't been eating,' the second nurse said.

'Okay, let me write down the volume of the vomit and I will call her doctor.'

The nurse looked at me and said, 'I'll be back soon, okay?'

I felt disorientated and ill. I waited for them to return but before they could my mouth began watering again. I looked to my side table – I still had another bowl. I grabbed it and held it in my hand just in case. Before long, I was throwing up the same green, bitter sludge into the bowl. The nurses came to write down the volume of green sludge and to bring a flesh supply of vomit containers, before helping me change and get more comfortable.

'We spoke to your doctor. He has advised we give you an injection for the nausea and vomiting, as well as something for pain and to hydrate you until he gets here.'

I nodded desperately. At that point, I would take anything if it made me feel a little bit better. After she had gotten rid of soiled clothes and bedding, she brought along her table of supplies to administer my medication.

'Let's start off with the anti-nausea stuff first, hey?' she asked. I nodded in approval.

As she looked up at the drip, adding new medication, she said to me, 'I think you might get moved to ICU today.'

I looked at her confused and at a loss for words. Again? How much longer would I have to be in ICU? I hated being in ICU for obvious reasons but another aspect that just unnerved me was being watched 24/7. Depending on how full the ICU was, a nurse would be assigned to one or two patients within close proximity to each other. They would sit at the end of the beds on a high chair, with a table that sloped downward towards them. Their notes were large sheets of paper wherein they documented every single thing. It felt so strange to open your eyes in the dimmed night lights to find someone watching over you and making notes.

Later that afternoon the catering staff had brought me a tray with a jug of fresh icy water, some juice, condiments, a knife, fork and spoon, a clean glass, some jelly and custard, and a plate covered with a heavy blue plastic lid.

'Thank you so much,' I said, even though I wasn't sure whether I would actually be able to eat anything while in such pain.

I lifted the lid and found some grilled white fish, some potato wedges and a grilled vegetable medley. It looked delicious. I tried to take a few bites but the pain intensified and the nausea started again. I poured myself some water and sipped on that.

Dr Blaauw stopped by and said, 'Oh good, you are eating?'

I said, 'Not really, I tried to take a few bites but I am in pain.'

He looked at my charts as I spoke. He looked back up at me and said, 'That's okay, at least just try when you can, even small bites.'

I nodded.

'So, Nadine, I am not going to beat around the bush,' he started. My heart started to thump in my chest; this couldn't be good. 'We found some issues in your X-ray and CT scan. On your X-ray, both of the bottom halves of your lungs have collapsed.'

'My lungs? How?' I interjected.

'Well, due to inflammation in your abdominal cavity. Your CT scan shows that your bowels are adhering to each other and that is why you have all these symptoms.'

I felt myself getting teary-eyed. 'So, what does this mean now?' I asked him as he stood at my feet.

'It means you need to go ICU for care but we are getting a team together because unfortunately we will have to operate again to release the bowels from each other.'

I was in disbelief. How could this be happening to me? I must have the worst luck in the world.

'An additional issue we are looking at is that there are clear infection markers. Your CRP rate tripled overnight since being admitted. We need to use appropriate antibiotics and treat the infection as well as remove things like abscesses.'

I shut down completely. I didn't respond; I had nothing more to say and I just felt so defeated. Dr Blaauw let me know a bed would be available later that afternoon and then I would be moved.

Once he was gone, with the curtains still covering me, I sobbed and didn't care who heard me. I couldn't believe this was happening to me again. Someone poked their head through the curtain and asked, 'Can I come in?' It was Melissa. In between sobs I said okay.

She didn't need much of an explanation and had heard most of what Dr Blaauw said. Instead, she just sat there with me and hugged me when I needed it.

I called my mom to let her know they were transferring me to ICU and it seemed I needed another surgery. 'Also, both bottom halves of my lungs have collapsed because of the inflammation,' I told her.

Each new piece of information left my mom shattered. She was scared and in a different city – flying to and fro for us as a working-class family just wasn't possible. I knew if she could have been by my side night and day she would have been. I just felt so fearful because I deemed ICU a place where people die. I had already been twice – was this going to be the time I didn't survive?

An older Indian woman had been moved next to me that morning. She had eavesdropped on everything my doctor and I discussed. 'How old are you?' she asked me. I told her but didn't know why she wanted to know.

'Wow, you are still so young. You know, I heard everything your doctor said and if I were you I would not go have another surgery.'

I just looked at her, trying not to be rude. 'He is just doing what's best for me,' I asserted.

She didn't seem to get the hint and went on and on about homeopathic medication. 'I think because of your age, rather get discharged and go the natural route because how many times will they want to cut you?'

I felt myself getting annoyed by her because if I could just leave and drink some holistic mengsel, I would have done that ages ago. I don't enjoy being in hospital or getting operated on.

She was still looking at me and said, 'And you know one day, you will want to get married and have babies, and then what are you going to do?'

It took everything in me not to tell her to voetsek; she was so invasive. Luckily for both of our sakes the porter showed up.

'I am looking for Ms Nadine Dirks,' he said.

'Here I am,' I said, eager to get away from the unsolicited advice and insensitivity. These surgeries were not elective and the husband-and-children comments always get under my skin.

Once I got settled in ICU, Dr Blaauw came by to let me know that he had arranged a team to work on me, a general surgeon, an endometriosis specialist, a bowel specialist, a urologist and a neurosurgeon to ensure all elements of the surgery would be handled well. Further, I would be seeing doctors in ICU daily to attend to my asthma and monitoring.

'When do I go into surgery?' I asked.

'Tomorrow morning, so, as you know, no eating and no drinking anything.'

I nodded. I was just so exhausted by the prospects of surgery.

Soon thereafter Dr Singh came by. 'Hi Nadine, I am Dr Singh. I just wanted to introduce myself to you because I will be assisting in your operation tomorrow.'

I studied him carefully. He seemed to be older which gave me confidence that he would have experience.

'Hi Doctor, so what do you do? What kind of doctor are you?' I asked him.

He smiled and chuckled at my curiosity. 'I am a general surgeon, which means I specialise in surgeries.'

Oh, that's interesting, I thought to myself. 'Sounds reassuring, Doctor. I will see you tomorrow.' I tried to sound brave.

After Dr Singh left, Dr Choonara, my urologist, stopped by. 'Hi Nadine, how are you? I was surprised to hear you were back here so soon after getting your stent removed?'

I felt quite sad because I too believed that removing my stent would be the last thing to deal with.

'I know, Doctor, I am surprised too,' I said.

'But, according to Dr Blaauw, you have been dealing with constipation for a while, even at the time you had your stent removed. Why didn't you say something?'

I thought about it carefully and looked him in the eye and said, 'To be honest, Doctor, I didn't think you'd care or think it was related. I also just assumed it was my endometriosis.'

He didn't seem to have much to say to me.

'Okay, we will see what's happening with you in the morning,' he said, without making eye contact.

'Okay, Doctor, see you then,' I said.

I was so traumatised by my last two hospital stints that this time I felt as if I was disassociating to keep myself sane; this time I didn't have my mom around either. I felt like this was truly it for me, that I have had too many near-death experiences to keep dodging death.

That night I found it hard to sleep. Although I was exhausted, medicated and depressed, I just couldn't seem to find any peace of mind to fall asleep. The room looked like the walls were closing in on me. I found myself crying silently. One of the nurses, Mam Joyce, must have noticed I was at breaking point. She came to sit with me, right next to my bed in a comfortable navy-blue chair, waiting for me to finally fall asleep. She was the gentle softness I desperately needed in that moment.

The following morning, I woke up completely frazzled and it hit me. I had to go into surgery again. I felt out of it, like I was losing my mind. I was crying incoherently, asking for help and searching for my mom. I begged the porter not to take me to the theatre floor. I was gasping for air as we arrived at the theatre. I felt like I was drowning. I was searching for air but it felt like I couldn't fill my lungs fast enough. My chest felt constricted, and I was still crying from the depths of my soul. I couldn't understand why this had to be happening. I was belligerent even towards people who were trying to help me. I was too panicked, afraid and traumatised to trust anyone or to be rational in that moment. If I could have pulled all the wires, tubes and intravenous lines out of my body and get up and walk away I would have.

I looked out of the window on my left side and it was still dark. I felt groggy, dazed and irritable. I just wanted to be left alone so I could sleep in peace. 'Wake up, Ms Dirks,' one of the nurses said. 'We have to get you ready so that you can get down to theatre on time okay.'

I remember trying to mumble no and shaking my head but they continued. One nurse looked at my notes and gathered them, another started unplugging all the machines attached to me, and the one who spoke to me tried to check if I had anything that needed to be removed before theatre. I felt so upset and scared, it was like I was in flight mode – I just wanted to get away and be left alone. I cried softly the whole way to the theatre waiting area.

My doctors came by to greet me. 'Don't be scared, it's going to be okay. We have a good team going in.'

I scoffed internally thinking to myself, well they've had good teams going in to do my surgeries and look how that turned out. I felt jaded and miserable – too much had happened in a short amount of time and I was shutting down mentally.

A nurse came and introduced herself. 'I will be inside with you the whole time as well,' she said.

I wish it brought me some sense of peace but still I felt myself struggling to breathe. The assistants came and wheeled me into theatre. I realised it was the exact same theatre space they had previously performed my surgeries in. I started to hyperventilate, screaming and crying hysterically, I kicked and screamed as they tried to transfer me from my hospital bed to the operating table. They got to work must faster than before – I guess so they could put me out and focus on the operation.

'I am so sorry, it's going to be okay, we will do our very best,' one of the doctors said to me.

The nurse who had introduced herself to me rubbed my arm gently. The anaesthesiologist put the cannula in my arm with such force because of his frustration with my anxiety attack that I yelped in pain. He didn't even manage to get it inserted correctly. A nurse took over and more gently inserted the cannula for the drip. Within minutes the area he had stabbed had already turned shades of blue and purple; it looked swollen. It felt like hundreds of people were around me. Everything felt like a blur. The last thing I remember was someone's hand putting a blue oxygen mask on my face as I desperately gasped for air, and then I was out.

Recovery 3.0

I FELT THE BRIGHTNESS OF THE fluorescent lights burning onto my closed eyelids as I struggled to open them and fully regain consciousness. I restlessly flayed my hands around in a state of distress. I still had the same feelings of panic that I had felt before I had gone under. I tried to feel my abdomen. It felt a lot more painful than just a keyhole surgery – my belly felt distended and hot and it hurt.

A nurse came over to wake me up. 'Wakey, wakey,' she said in a chipper voice.

I groaned both in response to her and the pain. I closed my eyes again and heard her request a porter. She came back to my bedside and said to me, 'You know the drill by now. We are going to send you to ICU because of your history.'

My eyes shot open in fear. I knew there was no point in protesting but I hated the ICU and everything that came with it. The porter came and took me back to not only the same ICU unit but also to the exact same bed I had been in the last time. My chest pounded just remembering what it felt like. The nurses gathered around me, plugging in all their machines and monitors, setting up my drips and medication. My eyelids felt like someone had poured cement onto them. I drifted off to sleep.

I was awoken by a sharp pain in my abdomen and a visit from the general surgeon. He seemed to be the kind of doctor who has seen it all and done it all, and had in the process become desensitised.

'Hi Ms Dirks, how are you feeling?'

Hearing so many people call me by my last name or even first name felt weird, it wasn't something I was used to since so many people have different names for me.

'Hi, Doctor. I am in pain, it feels hot and sore all over my abdomen,' I answered.

'I know, that's why I am here,' he said.

I looked at him puzzled.

'We started out doing a keyhole surgery but we had to abandon it because it took too much time and you weren't doing well, so we changed to a different incision,' he continued.

I was afraid to ask what he meant when he said I wasn't doing too well.

'What kind of incision did you end up doing?' I asked him.

He smirked at me playfully and said, 'Okay, so we went in and had to cut a midline incision, all the way up vertically, slightly above the belly button.'

I pulled a face and said, 'Ohh, that's why it feels like Satan has been using hot cleavers on my belly all day.'

He laughed and said, 'Yup! That'll do it.' He paused and then reminded me, 'We worked on your bowels, so it needs time to heal properly. You won't be able to eat solids for a while, and we will work our way up using things like soups, jelly and ice cream. For now, you will get everything you need from that.' He looked up and pointed at the giant bag filled with white liquid hanging above my head. I still had to continue with the antibiotics in the meantime to limit any chances of an additional infection or complication. I could feel I had a urine catheter inserted.

'Dr Singh, when can I have the catheter removed?' I asked.

'Oh, I am not sure, you will have to wait to speak to Dr Choonara who was also in the operating room. He decided it would be best to reinsert your stent due to all the inflammation and issues going on in your abdominal cavity, so I can't interfere with his stents.'

Ugh, this again, I thought to myself; one of the things I hated the most were the urine catheters. I couldn't fathom why I needed another stent inserted and hoped it was just a precaution and that nothing alternative had been noticed.

Dr Singh looked at me and said, 'You know, when we opened you up, you had three additional abscesses that we needed to drain, clean out and then wash your abdominal cavity with saline water again. Two were surrounded by inflamed tissue and one of them which was actually quite large was stuck in your bowel folds.'

I was surprised. 'That can happen?' I asked in disbelief.

'Yes, and it can make you incredibly sick. It is deadly if not treated. We also took some of the pus it contained to test and see which bacteria was involved so we can treat you with the right kinds of antibiotics instead of us just guessing.'

I was grateful that private healthcare had afforded me additional resources like fast-tracked bacteria cultures to avoid incorrect antibiotics, which would take up healing time and put further strain on my system if we didn't treat it properly. A nurse who had taken care of me before – Mme Tebogo – saw me as she was on her rounds. When she realised it was me, she came running towards me, smiling. She gave me the kind of hug that only a mom could give and said playfully, 'Ausi, what are you doing here again? If I find you here again I am going to give you a klap, ne!' before asking, 'What happened?'

I told her everything, how my bowels adhered to each other and how I was vomiting bile. She sat there next to me listening attentively. Mme Tebogo responded with a few 'batho ba Modimo', 'bathong lona' and 'no man's.

'But you know ne, ausi, every surgery, especially in the abdomen, has these exact risk factors. It is horrible and endometriosis is evil.'

I nodded and smiled at her. She had to go but promised to come by when she was able to. I was drained after all my visitors and had fallen asleep. I woke up feeling someone's presence next to me. It was a nurse I hadn't seen before.

'I just need to test your blood sugar and give you your meds,' she said listlessly.

I said okay and held out my left hand to her palm side up. She quickly pricked my middle finger and squeezed it to drip a droplet onto her testing strips. She shoved it into the machine and started tinkering with my drips.

'Can I please have something to hold on my finger, because it's still bleeding?'

She looked at me like I had asked her for the moon. She bent down and picked up a piece of tissue paper she had dropped earlier and handed it to me. I looked at it and looked at her, wondering if this was real. In what world does an ICU nurse hand you something from the ICU floor to put on your open needle pricks? I decided to just hold it on my hospital gown instead.

'Do you want your pain meds now or after I check your wound dressing?'

I thought about it quickly and said, 'After the wound dressing check.'

I didn't want to be conked out since I wanted to see myself and hopefully get a few photos to share with my mom so she knew what was happening and that I was okay. She moved my gown upwards gently. My belly was swollen and discoloured. The dressing was thick with multiple layers of gauze covered by a massive dressing. Although the gauze was thick, the dressing still seemed to be quite wet and slightly pinkish.

'Can you change it yet?' I asked the nurse.

'No, not on the first day,' she said.

I asked, 'Can I take a photo to show my mom?'

She looked confused by my request but answered, 'Sure.'

I took a few and put my phone down. In the meantime, she had set up new drips.

'Are you ready for your morphine?' she asked.

I nodded,

'Where do you want it?' she asked me.

I pointed to my left shoulder and said, 'Here, please.'

She wiped my upper arm and injected it. My arm felt tender but, before I knew it, I was out like a light.

I was worried about work while in ICU. I hadn't really been able to be on my phone much, and I didn't know what they would have said beyond the call the director and I had the day I had been admitted. She had acted disappointed, which to me seemed like such a strange emotion to have. I worried about losing my job; I worried about the fact that since the surgeries and hospital stays had been ongoing I would not be getting paid while off sick. I was incredibly stressed and cried often because I just thought of the crushing debt. The thought alone made my stomach turn. I would be in debt until the day I died at this point. The weight of the financial strain made my recovery so much harder because I had to shoulder so many different worries that wouldn't wait until I was in a better space to deal with it.

I felt like things would be easier if I died instead because I had so much on my plate, including my health. I felt so lonely and hurt. There is often no support in ICU because of the nature of it – patients aren't able to support each other, chat and motivate each other; people are just too ill. I worried about how I would pay my rent and other everyday things once discharged; it was soul destroying.

Dr Blaauw came by to check in on me. He noticed I looked upset, and before I even explained he said to me, 'If that woman wants to know anything, she should call me, and not bother my ill patient. How will you heal?'

I started to cry because it dawned on me that I even looked stressed out. Dr Blaauw let me cry and said he was sorry for me. He expressed similar findings to what Dr Singh had reported. 'Your bowels were looped together and that caused a lot of issues, even with your lungs because the pressure of the inflammation pushed your lungs. We removed everything and cleaned it out.'

I nodded and asked, 'What did the CT scan show?'

'Ah, okay, we found that at least there was no urine leakage this time, but you did have a high-grade left kidney infection. You also had an abscess, which was visible, in your left paracolic gutter. It was 2.5 cm by 1.8 cm in size, while the other two weren't visible on the scan.'

I tried to ensure I understood and remembered what he was saying. 'What is a paracolic gutter?' I asked.

'It is the space on the sides of your lower abdomen on the sides of your lower colon,' he responded.

I tried to envision it in my head. 'So why did the team change from a keyhole surgery?' I decided to ask Dr Blaauw after also speaking to Dr Singh – perhaps they had different thoughts.

'It was easier to see what we needed to do and to work fast since your vitals before weren't so good,' he explained. 'Everything went well, your ureter was easily restented, and Dr Singh is a great surgeon. He did a process called enterolysis which means he separated and removed a bowel loop in your pelvis.'

I looked at Dr Blaauw confused. 'In my pelvis? Not higher up? The pain felt higher up?'

He smiled and gently explained, 'Yes, the bowel in your pelvis was where the adhesions were, likely because of all the endometriosis we had to remove there. Endometriosis can be almost sticky so it easily attaches itself to other things and it creates equally as complicated scar tissue and adhesions when removed.'

I nodded again and asked, 'But why did I feel the pain so high up?'

He patted my arm and said, 'Because the inflammation was so severe, and because you also had two previous big surgeries and your kidney was badly infected. So, you would feel pain all over your abdomen.'

I smiled and thanked him.

'Rest, mobilise and get well soon, so you can go home.'

The nurse assigned to me came by with a trolley of things. It looked like wound dressing, gauze, medication and a big metal bowl with what looked like some water in it.

'Good evening, ausi, would you like me to help you bathe a bit?'

Ordinarily the idea of someone else helping to bathe me would make me cringe but this time I felt like it was a blessing.

'Yes, please,' I answered.

'I also have fresh linen for your bed.'

I smiled and said, 'But I can't get up sister, so I don't know if we can make the bed.'

She grinned at me exposing her beautifully straight teeth with gold caps. 'Hah! You'll see mntanam.'

She closed the curtains and got to work. She started with my face first, gently washing it with a white waslap. 'You have beautiful skin, it's so smooth,' she said as she wiped the soapy water off. She thought aloud, 'Should I wash you completely and then change the dressing or do it now and then wash you... hayi no the water will get cold.' Can I open the gown?' she asked as she wiped down every part of my body as gently as you'd handle a baby. Once she finished she said, 'Okay, do you trust me?'

I looked at her alarmed and said, 'I think so, why?'

She said, 'I am going to turn you on your side, then quickly wash and dry your back, but also remove the sheets and put new ones on.'

I looked at her like she had lost her mind. How was she going to do all that?

'Which side do you prefer to turn on?' she asked me.

I couldn't decide and said, 'It doesn't matter, it hurts both sides.'

She nodded and said, 'I will work fast.'

She put up the railings on the left side, gently rolled me onto my side, and asked me to hold onto the railing. She washed and dried my back, and slipped on a clean gown in seconds.

'Are you okay?' she asked.

'Yes, but hurry it's hurting more the longer I stay like this.'

She pulled the sheet off on the sides that were free and put the fresh sheets on halfway, she then gently turned me over onto my back. 'We are going to do the other side, it will be shap shap because I don't have to wash you or put a gown on. Do you want to take a small break?'

I smiled, out of breath, and said, 'Yes, please.'

She picked up the linen and gown she had removed, throwing them into a white plastic bag. She looked in my toiletry bag and found some moisturiser and gently applied it to my face and body.

'Okay, mntanam, are you ready now?'

'Yes,' I said nervously.

She gently rolled me to the left side and quickly slid the sheet on before turning me back.

'That wasn't so bad,' I remarked.

'I told you!' she said enthusiastically.

She used the remote on the side of the bed to move me into more of a sitting position. She put some toothpaste on my toothbrush and put a towel over my chest so I didn't mess on myself. She handed me the toothbrush and a kidney-shaped bowl to hold as I brushed my teeth. I spat out the extra toothpaste into the bowl and she handed me some water in a tiny plastic cup to rinse my mouth.

'Thank you so much,' I said. 'I feel like a human again.'

She beamed at me and said, 'Any time.'

As she gathered the used things on her tray, she said she'd be back. I realised I didn't know her name. When she returned, she had her tray again but this time just with my medication and wound dressings. As she walked in I asked her, 'Sister, what is your name?'

She smiled and said, 'It is Nomonde, you can call me Sister, MaNomonde, Mama Nomonde, Sr Nomonde, whatever you like.'

I liked MaNomonde most. She lifted the gown to examine the dressing. It hadn't been changed yet. She put on blue gloves and gently lifted the adhesive dressing. She threw the whole dressing away into a yellow bag she had attached to her trolley. MaNomonde noticed it was still oozing and quite swollen.

'I will make a note, but I am surprised that it is still oozing liquid, especially since you have a drain attached.'

She cleaned the area with saline and gauze, gently rubbing at bits of caked on fluids. Then she got some clean gauze and saline and cleaned down the line of staples. Some oozed a pinkish liquid as she wiped.

I looked down and said, 'MaNomonde, is that blood coming out?'

'No, baby, it's not, it's normal to have some discharge after surgery, it just seems like a lot but I will make a note.'

I asked her if I could take a photo for my mom. 'Of course, let me move my hand.'

She finished cleaning and applied more gauze on the long line of staples from my bikini line all the way past my belly button. She applied an adhesive wound dressing over the gauze and said, 'There you go! Now for pain medication, and then you will sleep well.'

I thanked her again. I was grateful for the help but also for the distraction from all the issues at work, with money and being away from my family while sick.

Recovery from surgery is hard and I had just had three. I have never hated jelly so much – it was my primary meal for most of my ICU stints. I felt hopeless; I just wanted to get out so badly.

Dr Choonara stopped by to see me. 'How are you?' he asked me.

'I guess okay. Can we take the catheter out yet?' I asked immediately.

He chuckled, saying, 'I knew you would ask me that! Unfortunately, we can't just yet. Your kidney infection was severe and as we know it has already been quite affected by the past surgery and endometriosis, so it is best that we keep the stent in while you recover, and I think it's best that the catheter stays in to help the healing process.'

I sighed, I just want to go home, I thought to myself.

He looked through my notes and said, 'Keep it up, okay?' before walking off.

The ICU unit felt strange, nurses almost seemed to be moving slowly, whispers abounded, something was wrong but I couldn't figure out what just yet. The interesting thing about being in an environment like an ICU is that healthcare providers often don't see you there and tend to speak freely. A nurse I hadn't seen before came to my bed, read my notes and said, 'Oh, you need your wound dressing changed again. Doctor said twice a day.'

She walked off to get the supplies. When she returned I asked her, 'Why do we have to change my dressings twice now? Shouldn't it be getting less?'

She looked in a daze and said nothing for a second. 'Uhm, because your wound is still quite wet and it keeps it from healing if we don't keep it dry,' she answered.

She sanitised her hands, threw on some gloves and asked to lift my gown to get to the wound. She took the old dressing off and started to grab gauze and saline, when another nurse barged in suddenly. She was chubby with her braids in a bun.

'Bathong, Sister, is it true?' she asked in surprised. The other nurse continued to clean the wound with saline and said, 'Yes, it is,' in a sombre tone. I tried to infer but I could feel it was something godawful. 'How did it happen?' she asked as the nurse dried my wound with gauze.

'Eish, sis, they say he did it here at his doctor's rooms, he shot himself in the head.'

I froze, unaware of who they were talking about, but focused on how terrible that was.

The nurse with the buns said, 'I cannot believe Dr Visser is gone. I worked with him just two days ago, he seemed fine, he didn't seem depressed.'

I felt chills. Dr Visser was one of my ICU doctors since my first time in the ICU; I saw him every single day except for weekends. I couldn't believe what I was hearing – he was pivotal to my healing. The lump in my throat grew bigger. How many more losses could I experience? How could so many people just be passing away all at once. It was too much to take in; I had to put it in a box in my brain or else I would break down.

The ICU ward remained sombre and the nurses spoke in hushed voices for a while.

I started to mobilise with the help of a physiotherapist in ICU. He would come by each morning around 10 and unplug everything aside from my oxygen tank and the ugly urine bag. We walked around the ICU slowly, with him holding my oxygen tank and me holding onto the urine bag. 'Not so fast,' he would tell me if I was overly eager to walk faster. 'Remember you haven't walked in a bit and we don't want you to get dizzy or to fall.'

After walking he would sit me in the chair for a while. 'You don't have to do anything, but I just want you to sit up for a bit.'

He handed me a plastic apparatus with a red ball inside. 'You have to blow and move the ball. Do this as often as you can.'

It seemed tedious and it was quite challenging.

'Why?' I asked.

'It will help with your lungs – getting them back to operating smoothly.'

I figured no matter how tedious, if it meant getting my lungs better, that would be one step closer to getting out of ICU and going home.

On weekends, there were often fewer staff members on rotation. I was assigned to a male nurse. I felt uncomfortable but tried to tell myself they are healthcare professionals and I shouldn't feel uneasy.

He was tall and wore a body warmer. He came by and introduced himself as Neo. 'I will be taking care of you today,' he said.

I smiled politely.

It was time for Neo to clean my wound and give me my pain medication. He came back with the supplies, setting them on my bed. He was chatty and friendly but I was unwell and in pain. I wasn't really in the mood for small talk; besides he made me quite uncomfortable – he would stand beside me at my head looking down as he cleaned the wound. It was different from others who stayed on the side of my bed, adjacent to the wound.

'Where are you from?' he asked me.

'Cape Town,' I said.

He seemed intrigued. 'I've never been there, you must show me around. Do you live here?'

'I live here now because of work,' I answered in a monotone.

'Oh, shap, let me know if you need me to show you around here in Jozi,' Neo said.

I didn't know how to respond without seeming like I was being snaaks. I felt uneasy and unsafe but how could I explain why? When he finished with my wound dressing, I covered myself in my gown quickly. It felt strange having a man cleaning the top of my pubic area. He removed my empty medicine bags and replaced them.

'Okay, so where must your injection go?' he asked me.

He was still at the top of my bed, by my head. 'In my arm,' I said and lifted my left arm to show him which one. He injected the morphine and I soon felt drowsy. My eyelids were heavy and I was ready to pass out when I felt the sensation of someone cupping my left breast. I passed out from the medication. When I woke up, I tried to recall what happened and if I was losing my mind. I put it down to the morphine – it had to be.

The next day I got a WhatsApp from a strange number. It read, 'Hello Nadine, this is Neo, I was your nurse the other day. I like you, even if you want as a big brother, hit me up.' I was in disbelief. Was a nurse seriously trying to hit on someone who was in ICU? A patient of his? I didn't recall giving him my number either. I felt physically ill. I decided to respond: 'How did you get my number?' I prised. He sent laughing emojis and said, 'Eish … it was on your information in your file.' I realised in that moment that maybe it wasn't the medication or my imagination; this man's behaviour was utterly inappropriate – he was invasive enough to steal my personal information. So maybe it wasn't so farfetched that he did in fact cup my breast, assuming I wouldn't know. Getting sexually assaulted in ICU is so bizarre and horrendous. People are often unconscious or on medications that knock them out. You expect to be safe; you expect that healthcare providers are there to help you. It was my worst nightmare come to life.

I didn't know what to do. I worried people would think I was lying or that I was misconstruing his behaviour; besides I also didn't really want to talk about it. It was another thing to add to the box of things I was unable to process and deal with without losing my damn mind. I felt like I wanted the skin of my body removed; I felt gross and like I needed to get rid of his touch on my body.

My doctors came by to see me and look at my file for updates. They agreed I could finally have the catheter removed and that I could be moved to a regular ward. I smiled widely – I was getting out – it was the best news I had gotten in a while. I would still need to continue with medication until I was stable, but I was given the go ahead to start eating soft foods like cooked veggies, mashed potatoes and eggs. Dr Singh asked to look at my wound himself. The nurse removed the soiled dressing to show the doctors. They discussed amongst themselves for a while before Dr Singh turned to me and said, 'Your wound is still quite wet and oozing. We will have to monitor that and keep changing the dressing up to three times a day.'

I wasn't too concerned; I was still in a euphoric state since hearing I could leave ICU.

'Okay, Doctor, that's fine,' I said.

The new ward was beautiful and modern. It was newly renovated and looked fancy. The room I was allocated to was quite large, and it was just me in the room. I enjoyed the silence, open space and not seeing other people. Soon after I had settled in, a woman was rolled in. She was groggy and groaning in pain. She didn't seem completely alert and kept making noises as if to clear her throat. I knew that sound; I got up and went to the nurses' station and requested a jug of water with ice and a glass. I hurried back and went to her bedside. I set the jug and glass down before pouring some water in a glass.

'Here you go, it's some cold water.'

She opened her eyes and looked at me curiously. 'How did you know?' she asked me.

I smiled and said, 'I have had many surgeries. I know how thirsty you can get and sometimes you have a little bit of throat irritation from the breathing tube.'

She smiled and chugged the water. 'Thank you so much,' she said.

That evening a few nurses came into the room and let me know that they needed to move me to a room next door with some other women.

'We need another room for men, everything else is occupied because of COVID infections.'

I nodded.

They gathered my things; one nurse carried it to the next room, the other removed my drip from above me, and they got ready to move my bed into the full room next door.

Everyone seemed quite nice; an older woman was opposite me, and another older woman to my right side, my bed was against the wall at the end of the room. I got up to get to my things but when I sat back down on the bed, it moved because the nurse had forgotten to set the brakes on my bed. It rolled backwards and pulled on my chest port. It didn't hurt too badly but the other women looked at me in shock. The one woman called for a nurse. I was confused by their reaction until I looked down. I was covered in blood and it was dripping onto the white linen, I tried to see where it was coming from to put pressure on it while the nurses came.

'Oh my goodness,' one nurse came running in. 'Askies! We didn't set the bed!' she said as she tended to the port, shutting it to stop the bleeding.

'Askies, yhu, askies,' she repeated.

'It's okay. Can I please have clean linen and a new gown?' I asked.

'No problem.'

The nurse hurried back. She put the clean linen on the wooden table at my bed and asked me to sit in the chair while she changed the bloody bedding.

'Can I help you bathe? Then you can change properly?'

I nodded and answered, 'Yes please.'

She helped me to the bathroom and helped me wash myself without getting the wound dressing wet again.

My wound still seemed to be seeping liquid – it kind of stained the wound dressing shades of yellow and pink depending on the day. The nurses continued to change it, but it still didn't seem to be helping. It was frustrating – the sooner it stopped, the sooner I could go home.

A new patient arrived. She seemed to be around her early fifties. She seemed delirious and she wasn't making sense. She would even speak in her state of sleep. It was annoying because she interrupted everyone else. 'My name is Jyoti,' she randomly announced. We shared our names with her and hoped that speaking to her would be helpful. She wouldn't let certain nurses touch her. She would scream bloody murder when they tried to check her vitals.

'They are trying to poison me. Why does she come to me first, she's evil and trying to find out my information.'

I asked, 'But why would she want to do that?'

Jyoti sat up in her bed and shared a strange story about when she was in the operating room for a scope. She said, 'They put me under anaesthesia, and when I woke up, I wasn't in the operating room, I was on a big round table with people around me waiting for my organs.'

The older woman across from me, MaBusi, and I shared a look. We couldn't understand what Jyoti was on about. She rambled incoherently to herself, and demanded the lights be on at night, which irritated everyone in the ward. I was so frustrated, I just wanted to go home. It felt like the other patients and I were left to deal with whatever was happening to Jyoti and it was disturbing.

One night she sat up on the side of her bed. I got up to go to the bathroom and found her sitting on the edge of the bed, mumbling. When she saw me, she said, 'Thank God, I can't sleep, it's so loud here, can you hear how they are partying outside?'

I asked, 'Who? Where are they partying?' I couldn't hear anything.

'The nurses and the doctors, they are partying and drinking, all night, I can't sleep,' she said again. I peeped my head out of the room door and couldn't see anything.

I decided to go to the nurses' station. A few nurses were there, busy with paperwork. I couldn't find the party and told the nurses what happened. They told me, 'No, she's mad in the head that one.'

Even so, I thought, she should have then been treated and monitored in a psych ward where there would be more understanding. I walked back to my room and told Jyoti I went to tell them to stop partying. She said, 'Thank you' over and over before going back to sleep.

My wound still soiled the dressings; the nurse seemed worried and unsure as to why it was happening. No one really said anything. They spoke around me, they spoke to each other, but not directly to me – it was frustrating because I knew that my wounds didn't take so long to heal. When the nurse came back after discussing the issue of my wound with another nurse, I asked, 'What's going on?'

She looked hesitant but responded by saying, 'It is taking longer than usual to heal so we are going to send you to a wound specialist called Sr Lorna.'

It sounded good to me. I knew if my wound was healthy, they'd send me home.

The nurse made plans for me to see Sr Lorna. I assumed she was somewhere in the hospital when the porter came by with a wheelchair. The nurse said, 'Take your folder along.'

I got into the wheelchair and he pushed me to the lifts and we travelled down to the ground floor. I was in a hospital gown and the air felt chilly. The porter asked me to sit and wait in the wheelchair while he went to look for someone to take me to Sr Lorna. He went outside and I wondered what he was doing outside. I looked down and noticed my blue hospital gown was wet around the wound area.

He couldn't come back fast enough. The porter pushed me outside and helped me into a cart. I struggled to get in because of the height and small space. I was worried because it was cold and I wasn't dressed for the cold or to be outside.

The driver told me not to worry and that Sr Lorna was the best. We got going all the way out of the hospital's main entrance, bouncing our way over speed bumps. I was anxious and scared. Why were we exiting the hospital's grounds; how far was this place? I held onto the bar in front of me firmly, watching my knuckles turn white from the force. I tried not to fall and hurt myself. Eventually we arrived at a centre on the right side of the hospital. I noticed a Steers sign, dentists and optometrists and even an electronic store inside. The driver of the cart helped me get out and grabbed a wheelchair from inside the centre to put me in.

The building seemed quite old and dilapidated; the lift made loud noises on its way down to us. People stared at me as the driver wheeled me in – I am sure I must have looked a sight. We got into the old lift and made our way to Sr Lorna's office.

Her gate was locked but her door was open. It was quiet with no one in the reception area. The driver knocked and shouted, 'Sr Lorna, I have a patient here.'

Sr Lorna flew around the corner with a set of keys jingling in her hand. She had a short blonde afro and seemed very friendly and talkative.

'Oh my goodness, John, I am so sorry, I was in the back, sorry to keep you waiting,' she said as she opened the gate. The driver whose name I now knew was John wheeled me in and said, 'I will wait downstairs, sisi.'

Sr Lorna smiled at me broadly. 'I have been waiting for you to arrive all afternoon!' she said.

She handed me a form to sign before helping me out of the wheelchair to go to her office. It was a large room, with two beds, a sink, a desk and a wall with cupboards stacked with boxes on the top. The windows seemed small for the size of the room.

She helped me onto the bed while chatting to me, asking how I was doing, and if I knew why I was there to see her. Once she lay me down she went to her sink and thoroughly washed her hands before drying them and putting on gloves. She had her metal tray ready to go and asked if she could lift up my gown.

'Eish ... this looks sore. Is this always like that?' she asked, pointing to a section of my lower belly that was quite round.

'Yes, I guess so, but it looks extra puffy since there is an incision separating my lower belly in the middle.'

She nodded and continued to examine my wound. She pressed on certain places, moved my skin and measured the size of the wound.

'Can I take a photo?' she asked.

I looked at her for a second, unsure as to why she wanted a photo. She piped up and said, 'It's just that sometimes if we don't document everything, medical aids refuse to pay for the services and say it wasn't so bad.'

'Oh, in that case, sure,' I answered.

She put a disposable ruler on my belly and took a photo.

'There we go,' she said.

She got some gauze and saline to clean the wound. 'What have the nurses been doing every day with regards to wound care?' she asked without looking up, still cleaning in between each crevice and staple.

I thought about it and said, 'Uhm, they clean it with gauze and saline and then they put the wound dressing back on.'

She looked up at me over her red framed glasses. 'Seriously?' she said. 'That's absurd. There is obviously an infection here.'

I panicked, thinking I couldn't deal with another infection.

'Infection?' I asked in distress.

Sr Lorna stopped and looked at me and said, 'Yes, it is an infection, but on the skin, not inside, so it is not as dire and all we need to do is ensure we dry up the liquid completely to keep it from being wet and we add some medicated ointment and close it up and it'll resolve, okay?' she said.

'Okay,' I answered.

Sr Lorna grabbed some kind of metal tool after cleaning the wound. 'There are too many staples; it's not allowing the liquid to come out at once and keeping certain areas more wet than others,' she announced.

I lay back, looking at the ceiling and the bright light above my abdomen.

'Is it okay? I need to remove some of the staples, it shouldn't hurt,' she asked me.

'If the doctor says it's fine, then it's fine by me, as long as it won't burst open,' I said, laughing.

'Well, your doctor suggested coming to see me, so they won't have an issue,' she assured me as she started to remove every alternate staple. It felt less tight and painful than before.

I smiled and said, 'Thank you so much, it feels so much better and not so tight.'

Sr Lorna smiled back and grabbed a big box.

'I want to show you something,' she said as she tried to open the box. As she wrestled the box, she said, 'I think we should do a vacuum dressing for you. That way you don't have to worry about constantly changing the dressing, or getting it wet, and it will speed up the healing time.'

Eventually she got the box open and showed me a new vacuum machine, which would be mine. I had never had one before. It looked about the size of a camera. It sounded extraordinary but how does it work? I wondered.

As if she were reading my mind, she said, 'So, how it works is, we put a dressing on your wound, which has a pipe attached to it that feeds into the machine, the machine has a backend filled with a type of material that catches the liquid and absorbs it. You have to charge the machine. It stays on you at all times and needs to constantly be suctioning,' she explained while holding the machine up so I could see what she meant.

'What if it gets full? Or if the dressing doesn't seal perfectly?' I asked her.

She smiled and said, 'Don't worry, I will give you my WhatsApp number. You will come see me every three or four days. If it's full then we just put in a new filter, and I will make sure it's suctioned well. I will also give you extra wound dressing to add wherever you find it is not sealing well.'

She looked at me with empathy and said, 'Don't worry. The machine will let you know by beeping if it is not suctioning and you will feel the difference, and it will show a red light and beep when it needs to be charged.'

I nodded and felt assured as she dried the area and added the dressing onto my abdomen. It covered the wound well. She then added additional transparent wound dressings to keep everything secure so the suction would work well. She adjusted the machine settings before attaching the tube to the machine, made a few notes and then took a black bag out of the box.

'Here is your designer bag,' she joked. 'You can put the machine in here. The bag has an open section around the tube so you can have it in your bag and move around easily without carrying it.'

I looked at everything, trying to take it all in so I didn't forget anything. Sr Lorna turned the machine on and it instantly started to suction away. I was impressed by the entire process and felt a lot better that the wound wasn't going to be constantly open and exposed. Sr Lorna helped me up and called John to come back. She helped me to my wheelchair and handed me my folder, hanging the bag around my neck so I didn't have to hold it in my hands. Great thinking since being in the back of a cart, in a hospital gown, holding a folder and a machine didn't seem like a good idea.

I was eager to get back to the ward to sleep. Little did I know, I would be met by chaos from Jyoti when I got back. She was in a state, ranting randomly and I was unable to follow anything she was saying. I asked MaBusi in Zulu, 'Kwenzakalani?' to which she raised her brows, pursed her lips and said, 'Angaz', sisi, it's been going on since uhambile.'

MaBusi and the other patients seemed annoyed. It was around dinnertime, and Jyoti's odd behaviour appeared to get worse at night. We couldn't figure her out and she didn't have any visitors who we could have made aware of her odd behaviour. She would kick and scream as if she were fighting someone; she especially targeted certain nurses.

I covered myself in my blankets – I was quite cold from the trip back to the hospital. Jyoti's sights fell on me and she said, 'Hey you!'

I wasn't sure who she was talking and so didn't answer.

She shouted louder, 'Hey you!'

I looked at her and said, 'Are you talking to me?'

'Yes, your name is Jill, I remember you,' she said, smiling at me.

I thought about it for a second. 'No, my name is not Jill. I don't know anyone named Jill. My name is Nadine,' I responded firmly.

She looked dishevelled and said, 'Yes, you are. We used to work together, remember? You are my coloured friend. You look like my coloured friend.'

MaBusi uttered, 'Haibo.'

I was stunned into silence and didn't know what to say since she didn't seem well. I just smiled at her, although I felt annoyed by her lowkey racist comments, not to mention the fact that she was loud and disruptive. One of the other patients got up to go to the bathroom. When she reached out her hand to open the door, Jyoti screeched so loudly we all turned to look at her. The woman froze at the bathroom door, confused. She turned to look at Jyoti too. Jyoti screamed at her in a high-pitched voice, 'Don't go in there, don't go!'

The woman asked, 'Why not?'

Jyoti looked at her with fear in her eyes and said, 'Password and Wi-Fi are hiding in the bathroom, don't go in there, they've been in there all day.'

We all stared at her, wondering who on earth Password and Wi-Fi were, how they managed to sneak into a small bathroom stall comfortably, and why they were there to begin with. The woman reached out again to open the door, this time to see what was happening. Jyoti's bed was right opposite the bathroom. She screamed in horror when the woman went into the bathroom and we all waited to hear what the issue was when the woman came out.

After a minute or so, we heard the toilet flush and then the sound of the tap, before she opened the door. She walked out normally and nothing seemed different. Jyoti stared at her in fear again, but this time, she seemed terrified of the woman too.

MaBusi sat up in her bed and asked the woman, 'So what was in the bathroom?'

She scoffed and said, 'There is nothing there; I don't know what she's on about.'

We decided to call a nurse, since we all had to go to the bathroom badly but we didn't want to continue traumatising Jyoti. When the nurse arrived we told her about Password and Wi-Fi who were hiding out in our bathroom and that Jyoti feared for her life.

The nurse pulled Jyoti's curtains closed so that she could inspect the bathroom without Jyoti being in full view. The nurse looked everywhere, even in the cistern, and found absolutely nothing. She came out and opened Jyoti's curtains and sat down on the side of her bed.

'I didn't find anything in the bathroom, so I think it's fine and you're safe,' the nurse said.

Jyoti looked towards the bathroom and said, 'They are hiding; they like to do that to me.'

The nurse didn't argue but asked her, 'So what will we do if you need to go to the bathroom?'

They settled on adult diapers to make it easier.

All the Password and Wi-Fi drama had made me forget about my new device. It seemed to be working well, the catchment area seemed to have some waste in it and my wound dressing wasn't seeping liquid anymore. I was delighted. I was one step closer to getting home.

Dr Singh came by the evening to check in. 'I heard you saw the miracle worker Sr Lorna? How did that go?' he asked.

I smiled and said, 'It was great, she gave me a vacuum dressing, and already I can tell the dressing doesn't seem to be drenched in liquid. She also removed a few staples so now it doesn't feel as tight.'

He smiled and nodded. 'Can I see the wound and the vacuum dressing?' he asked.

'Sure,' I said and showed him the machine and moved my gown so he could see the dressing. He looked at everything intensely. He looked at my folder and back at the dressing.

'Hmm, it seems you are doing really well, and if you have the wound vac then we can let you go home sooner because we don't need you to be in hospital for daily dressing changes to avoid further infection,' he said.

I felt teary with excitement. 'When can I go home?' I asked.

He looked at my folder again and said, 'Saturday is your next wound change. It's important for Sr Lorna to see if it's working, if it needs anything else, that kind of thing so I would rather wait for her to see you on Saturday and if she is happy then you can go home with your wound vac.'

Saturday was only two days away. I just had to hold on a little bit longer and hopefully nothing else would go wrong that needed me to stay longer. I was scheduled to see Sr Lorna in the afternoon, so I asked my friend Jamil to be on standby in case they finally decided to let me go home.

On Saturday morning, while breakfast was being served, Sr Lorna marched in with her little black duffle bag. She was cheerful and greeted everyone on her way to my bed. She put her bag down and said, 'Hello! I was coming in here anyway, so I thought I might as well come see you here.'

I smiled broadly, 'Yay, I am so glad because Dr Singh said everything looks good, and the wound vac means I can go home and not worry about daily wound dressing changes and infections.'

She opened her bag up and asked if she could see my abdomen and the machine.

'Okay, this is good. Lots of fluid came out. We can change the cartridge so that you can go home with a new one. I will change the dressing now so I can see how it looks.'

Sr Lorna was gentle. She used some kind of smelly liquid that helped the dressing lose its adhesive strength so she didn't have to tug on my skin. She put all the soiled dressings into a special bag to be discarded. She then changed her gloves and started to clean the wound.

'It looks good, Nadine, I'm really happy.' She asked if she could take some more photos for her records and I said, 'Of course. Does this mean I can finally go home?'

She looked up at me as she took a photo and said, 'Yes, I think it's fine.' She smiled.

When she finished my dressing, she used the call button at my bed to call the nurse. When the nurse arrived, Sr Lorna told her, 'Please prepare this patient's discharge for today. Her doctor's cleared her and she will see me every three days or so as an outpatient.'

The nurse said okay and left to begin the process.

I could hardly believe it. I sent a message to my family and Jamil to let them know that I was being discharged. I was so excited I couldn't even eat breakfast. I immediately got my bag out and started putting away all of my things. I went to the bathroom and got changed into some tracksuit pants and a hoodie. All I needed to do was wait for my meds to be brought to me, sign some forms and wait for the porter.

Getting my house in order

GETTING HOME AFTER SO long was so refreshing. Jamil had taken it upon himself to do my laundry, change my bedding, clean my kitchen, tidy my bedroom and ensure the space was comfortable for me when I returned. I beelined to my couch and sat down. Jamil turned on the heater and we discussed what we would do for the rest of the day like we always did. I felt human after such a long time and I revelled in it.

I still felt nauseous eating certain things after having bowel issues. Jamil and I decided to hop in the car with my wound vacuum in tow to go to Woolies for food and snacks my body wouldn't rebel against. I felt so normal walking around the store, taking it all in.

Under the surface I was still overwhelmed and worried about work; I knew that eventually I would have to make contact and I decided that on Monday I would let them know I had been discharged, but I had no idea what I was in for. I spent the weekend relaxing, hanging out with Jamil and, since I had the wound vacuum, I could even take a quick shower – as long as I didn't get the wound dressing soaked it would be okay. I took full advantage. I got a chair to put in the shower, and used it to balance as I washed myself from head to toe.

On Monday morning, I sent a short and simple email to the

director and my manager saying, 'Hello, I just wanted to let you both know that I am finally at home, although with a wound vacuum but nonetheless I am grateful to be home.'

I was hoping they would be glad for me and let me know that we could have a meeting to debrief so that I could start working from home as I recovered. Instead, I got an email from the director saying, 'I will call you soon.'

My stomach turned; I hated speaking to her because she made me incredibly anxious.

My phone rang barely 15 minutes later. I grabbed it anxiously, looking at her name on the screen for a second. I answered and said, 'Hello…'

Her tone was different this time around – she sounded way more formal than ever before. 'Hello, Nadine, thank you for letting us know you are home, how are you?' she asked me flatly.

'Uhm, I am as okay as I can be, thanks for asking. How are you?'

There seemed to be a lull in the conversation, as if she was trying to get through all the required niceties before letting me know what she was actually calling for. Eventually she piped up and said, 'We were speaking to HR and a few other people and they've agreed you are unfit for work.'

It was so matter of fact; as if I didn't need to be a part of the conversation. I felt myself completely dissociating. She babbled on but I hardly heard her in the background. I then asked, 'So what are my choices here?' I needed confirmation.

She waited a beat before answering, 'Well, we discussed that since you are unfit, we can declare you disabled and that way you can be home, or we can split ways mutually. The only issue with declaring you unfit to work is that you haven't worked long enough to get financial benefits.'

I teared up; my throat felt thick. I looked up to the ceiling to keep from crying and then answered, 'Okay, could HR look at potential financial benefits for me? Before I make any decisions?'

I was in disbelief, but part of me expected it.

'Sure, we can do that. But we will also need your decision soon, like I said we need a body in the role.'

I had a visceral reaction to her using the term 'body' again.

We exchanged a few awkward pleasantries before hanging up.

I felt like my world had stopped. I looked around at the apartment and life I had built in Johannesburg, knowing it would all be snatched away either way. I grabbed my phone to call my mom. I needed to vent and get her advice.

When I heard my mom's voice I broke down.

'What's wrong, what happened?' my mom asked me.

She sounded alarmed; I told her the director had called me.

'Okay, what did she say, my kind?'

I sobbed in between words and said, 'Mommy, she says that they think I am unfit and they gave me two choices.'

I heard my mom exhale into the receiver.

'Okay, what did the tief say are your options? Also is she a doctor now? Declaring you unfit for work! And she was being so nice kammalyk and told me your job was safe.'

I wiped my face with a folded stack of toilet paper, hoping to stop the tears.

'She says that either they can declare me unfit and I can see what benefits they have for me or I can separate amicably from them, but I asked them to check the benefits before I decide.'

My mom's voice changed. I could tell she was disturbed and upset hearing what happened. She said very quickly, 'No, no, no it doesn't even matter how much benefits they give. Basically that then means you are unfit to work even at another place, so it is not a win. I can't believe this kak, sy dink sy speel met fokken poppe.'

I was surprised and sobered up once my mom explained what unfit to work means. It made my head spin and it dawned on me that she had given me an impossible situation. I realised that what the director had said was true. I hadn't been working long enough for the benefits to be beneficial to me. 'So, what do I do now?' I asked.

She exhaled heavily again and said, 'This is a kak one because if you were better I would have suggested taking them to the CCMA but I know this isn't something you can do now. I don't know what to say, honestly. You know if me or Daddy could financially help, we would but we can't so I don't know what to say.'

I think she tried to shield me from just outright saying, 'You will need to come back home.'

I decided to push her for an answer because, to be honest, I needed someone else to help.

'I know, Mommy, but would you rather just separate or be declared unfit?'

She softly said, 'If it were me, I would rather separate because this issue is stressful enough on you and you need to heal.'

I nodded knowingly, 'Okay, Mommy,' I said.

We said our I love yous before ending the call. I sat on the couch staring at the wall for a good 30 minutes; it felt like my body couldn't move. The next morning, I got an email from the director. I immediately opened it. She was short and to the point: 'Hi Nadine, can you please take stock of all the items you have from work? Including laptops and work clothing. We have attached a list so please fill it out and send it back.'

I was annoyed by her. Do I really have to tally up every pen and pencil to make them comfortable? Besides it made it clear they had already decided I wasn't coming back.

I got ready for my appointment with Sr Lorna and decided I would do it later if I felt like it. Sr Lorna's office seemed busier than the last time. I signed in with the receptionist and sat down.

'Nadine, I will be with you shortly. This patient was sent over by the hospital urgently,' Sr Lorna said to me when she saw me in the waiting area.

The wound vacuum seemed to work well but the little vacuum seemed to fill up quickly. I also had thick bits stuck in the pipe that looked like some kind of pus or what I imagined fat looks; it freaked me out.

Sr Lorna wheeled the patient into the waiting area. 'Please call a porter for him, Tiffany,' she told the receptionist. She looked so different: she was wearing a hairnet, booties on her feet, with a light blue disposable jump suit.

'I will be with you in a few minutes, I just want to disinfect everything.'

I smiled at her, nodded and said, 'Okay, Sr Lorna.'

I went back on my phone and re-read the director's email in the meantime. It made my stomach hurt. In that moment I realised I would be mistreated if I fought for my job in any way.

I must have been in my own world thinking about how unfair the work situation was because I missed Sr Lorna calling me. On the second try she came closer and said, 'Nadine, I am ready for you. You can come through hey.'

I shot up and followed her.

She helped me onto the bed. 'Okay, there you go. So how has it been going?' she asked me, while putting on a pair of gloves.

'Uhm, I think it's been okay, just the machine seems to fill up fast, and there are these thick chunks that accumulates in the tube also.'

She nodded and smiled. 'Okay! Let's have a look. I also want to remove the rest of the staples, okay?'

I nodded.

She started to remove the now soiled dressing and looked at the tube and wound vacuum intensely before making a note. She looked at my belly and put a ruler beside the wound and asked if she could take photos again.

'Yes, you can take photos,' I said to her.

'It looks good and less swollen. I am happy with this,' she said, while lifting my hottentot apron up to view the rest of the wound. She started cleaning it with a liquid that smelled like Jeyes Fluid, before sitting down on a high chair beside me. She put her glasses on, moved her little silver trolley and said, 'Okay, now for the staples.'

She grabbed a metal tool and put a piece of gauze next to me, gently starting to remove the staples. It wasn't bad at all; it felt like a little bit of pressure and then it was out.

Sr Lorna put her glasses back down. 'Okay, so what I am thinking is, we can use a bigger machine this time, so it doesn't fill up too quickly. Even the wound dressing is longer so it will cover everything nicely.'

'Okay, that sounds good.'

She got up to wash her hands and get the bigger wound vacuum from on top of a row of cupboards. As she did that, she asked me where I was from.

'Cape Town!' I said.

She said, 'Oh my, that is surprising. I don't know many Capetonians who would move here. You guys love your city.'

I laughed. 'That's true, but I love Johannesburg, so I guess I am an outlier. Where are you from?' I asked her.

She came back towards me with the new wound vacuum. 'Durban, born and raised,' she smiled proudly.

She started to set the wound vacuum up, pressing buttons rapidly but still able to talk. 'Do you miss Durban?' I asked her.

She looked at me and said, 'Hmm, well I have been here for over twenty years, so it isn't so bad anymore. Lots of my family moved here and I had more opportunities here, so it's not so bad anymore.'

I watched her tinkering with the vacuum's settings. 'Ah, okay, that makes sense,' I said.

She happily announced, 'There we go! Perfect! I got the setting I wanted for you.'

She wheeled herself closer to me and said, 'Okay, let's attach it.'

She changed her gloves and poured some more dark foul-smelling liquid onto a chunk of gauze. She wiped the entire area again before putting on the giant wound dressing.

'Okay, now I have to concentrate and put this on the wound perfectly.'

She got it perfectly aligned and on with the precision of a

surgeon. She attached the tube to the wound vacuum and pushed a button to start the suctioning. It felt different than the smaller one, a little bit more intense.

'Sister, I am thinking of going home, so how does it work if I have a wound vacuum?' I asked.

'Oh, you're gonna go back home? Okay, when will you leave?'

I tried to count the days in my head. 'Uh, I think in eight or nine days from now.'

Sr Lorna nodded and said, 'Well, if you still need it, you can take it with you and I can refer you to another wound specialist, or it may be dry enough for us to take the wound vacuum off. We will see.'

I nodded and sighed in relief. As she finished off and made notes, I remembered the thick bits in the tube and realised I hadn't got an answer about it.

'Sister, what is the stuff in the tube that looks so thick?'

She chuckled and said, 'Don't worry about it, it happens. It's a mixture of things like skin cells, pus, blood cells and all kinds of things the vacuum pulls out, which is good – the less infectious matter sitting on your wound the better.'

I listened intently. 'Okay, good, that's good to hear.'

I started to get up with the help of Sr Lorna. 'Okay, darling, I will see you in four days or so; here is your Gucci bag.'

She handed me the vacuum in a big black bag. It felt quite hefty compared to the one I had before but I just wanted it to get everything out as soon as possible, so I made peace with the 'car battery' I had to lug around. It was particularly cruel in the middle of the night, when I would wake up to go to the bathroom and forget I was attached to this giant wound vacuum – although the hysterical beeping and vibrating at 2 am when it needed to be charged may just be the thing that drove me up the wall more than lugging it around everywhere.

When I got home from the appointment, I decided I needed to nap and didn't have the energy to search for everything from work for a stupid checklist. When I woke up, I noticed a missed call from the director.

'Ugh, I shouted. I knew she was calling about this dumbass checklist.

I got up and put the wound vacuum in its bag and put it over my shoulder. I went to my desk and opened the checklist. I ticked the boxes that contained items I knew I had off the top of my head, then started the search for the rest of things on the list, down to lanyards and washable face masks they had given us. 'This is the most ridiculous kak on earth; these people would want the cup of tea I had once back if they could request it,' I said aloud to myself. I searched high and low, making notes of each item down to quantities, while simultaneously packing the things up and putting them in the corner of the room, so I could just hand it over. I completed the checklist and sent it back to them with a simple note: 'FYI.'

I sat down, exhausted and sweaty, and with a few minutes I got an email from the director: 'Thanks, Nadine. Can I come by and fetch it perhaps this Saturday morning?' she asked.

I immediately responded and said, 'Yes, sounds good to me.'

About an hour later, I heard the email tone on the work laptop chiming, and I went over to see what else they had to say. It was an email from HR regarding my benefits. I opened the email eager to see what they could afford. My jaw hit the floor with a quickness: 'Hi Nadine, Samantha said that you asked her to get information regarding benefits if you decide to go with the option of being declared unfit. Unfortunately, you haven't worked here long enough to get any worthwhile benefits. It may just be a once-off amount of R8000. Let me know how you would like to proceed.'

Seeing the director's first name being used made me irrationally uncomfortable, as if it humanised her as an empathetic person when she isn't; Samantha was the opposite to me. I felt like I knew what I wanted to do in that moment – I wanted to go home. I didn't want to hear the back and forth and I didn't want to deal with paperwork and Samantha's bullshit.

I responded: 'Hi Helena, thank you for your email. Please can you prepare the paperwork for the mutual separation? Thanks.'

I cc'd Samantha too so she knew where I stood and hopefully would stop calling me without asking and speaking for 45 minutes. I felt relieved and free after emailing HR; I felt confident about my choice. I sat back and exhaled, smiling at my laptop. Although I had already signed the documents to go our separate ways, I still needed to hand over their belongings. I couldn't wait to hand over on Saturday and look Samantha in the face and tell her how awfully they treat people and that what they do is hostile and created a shitty work environment in general.

Saturday morning, I woke up at the buttcrack of dawn. I got myself ready and carried the stuff to the living room. I waited for a message or a call from her – morning was almost over. I wondered if maybe her morning had gotten super busy but I found it odd that she hadn't communicated anything. Around 1 pm I sent her a WhatsApp message: 'Hi Samantha, are you still stopping by for all your things?'

I waited for a response but around 3:30 pm it just felt unlikely that she would come. I decided to try and call her, but it just rang. I suspected she must have been awkward about seeing me in person again or what I would say, especially now that I had already signed the resignation letter and had nothing to lose.

On Monday I got an email from her. I rolled my eyes in advance, wondering what the excuse would be. I opened the email: 'Hi Nadine, I am sorry for not getting to you this weekend. Can you please ensure you drop everything off at the office this week?'

I sat there flabbergasted. She knew I still had a wound vacuum; I was still recovering. I didn't have a car and the things to return were a lot for one person to carry. I felt so angry and disgruntled – how in the fuck could she even expect that? At the height of the most dangerous wave of COVID, surely she didn't expect me to get into an Uber with a compromised immune system? I thought about it and settled on just letting her know the situation: 'Hi, well as you know I am still recovering and I don't have a car, so I will need to find someone to drive me to the office to drop it off.'

I hoped this would encourage her to offer an alternative solution that would take into consideration my situation. Instead, I got an email back saying, 'Okay, thanks, let us know beforehand when you will be coming to drop things off.'

I released a few choice words from my mouth like I was spitting out bile; I needed to get it off my chest. I got on WhatsApp and asked Jamil if he could drive me to the office sometime that week. He responded almost immediately: 'Sure, I can do Thursday?'

'Sounds good,' I replied.

I sent the director an email letting her know I would be coming around on Thursday morning. I was due to see Sr Lorna too and got a voice note from her the day before the appointment: 'Hi Nadine, I have tested positive for COVID this morning, so I won't be able to see you. Please look out for any symptoms of COVID on your end as well. I will ask Tiffany to get some new dressings, cleaning supplies and then I will guide you on a video call. You will need to do it yourself, I promise it will be easy. I will ask her to put extra dressings in for you. Okay, take care.'

Ugh, just what I needed, a potential COVID scare… I grabbed my phone to let Jamil know, since we spend a lot of time together. We both seemed fine and had no symptoms at least. I felt extra paranoid and worried, watching seemingly healthy people die from the third wave scared the life out of me. I kept looking out for the slightest tickle in my throat or cough. I counted down the days since I had seen Sr Lorna to calm me down and keep me from losing grip with reality.

I went to grab the supplies from Sr Lorna's office and sprayed it down at home. I washed my hands, took off the old dressing and put it in a plastic bag. I took a photo for Sr Lorna and started to clean the wound. Sr Lorna responded instantly: 'Looks good, let me give you a call now.'

My phone rang. I answered and Sr Lorna carefully talked me

through the process.

'You're doing a good job,' she would say with each step.

'Okay, a little bit to the left,' she said as she watched me try to centre the wound dressing.

'Okay, perfect, put it down onto your skin and rub out any air bubbles gently so it sticks perfectly.'

I felt my hands shake with anxiety. I did as I was told and by some miracle it looked pretty good.

'That's perfection! Now secure it, put the tube into the wound vacuum and turn it on,' she guided me.

'Okay, what happens if it doesn't suction?' I asked her.

'That's okay, then you can use the other smaller dressings as a plaster on the areas that aren't suctioning to secure them,' she said gently.

The vacuum started to rapidly suction as soon as I turned it on. Sr Lorna laughed gleefully like a child. 'Perfect! You did it, well done!'

I laughed nervously, still a little bit surprised that I managed to change the wound dressing myself. I headed to bed to watch some TV before going to sleep. I needed to be up early to go to the office to drop off the things. I was a little bit anxious because I didn't know what I'd be walking into.

I tossed and turned in some kind of weird dance wherein my eyes were closed and I tried forcing them shut tightly hoping it would convince me to switch off, but I felt the night turn into the morning. The light of morning slowly threatened to disturb my sleep charade. I opened my eyes in frustration and quickly hauled myself out of bed. I felt my anxiety filtering through my body like electricity, the dawn of a new day offending my blackout curtains. I grabbed the massive wound vacuum and went to the bathroom where I stood in front of the mirror staring at myself in a thick brown polar fleece pyjama set my mom had bought me for my birthday. My hair looked wild. I studied my face, looking for bits of myself that I recognised. I looked at the stranger staring back at me. Her face looked puffy, bruised; her eyes looked unusually wide like she was perpetually shocked; she was bleak. I felt my chest tighten, my heartbeat suddenly going into overdrive. I held onto the door for support and gathered myself before the tears could fall. I walked over to the living room – the tiles were icy beneath my bare feet – I sat down and dropped the wound vacuum on the floor. I looked at the bag of reminders of the job I had moved for, the job I enjoyed, the job that turned on me when I was unwell. I felt the anger rise in my throat like bile, and I felt hot with rage.

'Who would want a freaking worn T-shirt back?'

I opened the black plastic trash bag and looked at the contents once more, to make sure I had packed each thing listed. I figured that once I handed it over, I would express to the director how awfully they had managed me and my circumstances, not to mention treating me like a criminal all of a sudden when they didn't have a use for me.

I sat on the couch and stared at the bag for a while. I felt like it just couldn't be, it felt like someone tried to put me in that bag, like someone was attempting to walk away with the contents of who I am. My phone broke the trance. It sang louder and louder to wake me up. I grabbed it and put it off. It was time to get ready. Jamil would be here soon and I needed to be ready to go. I stood at the window of my bedroom, watching the cars go by. I looked out for Jamil so I could make my way down with my wound vacuum and the remnants of a job soured like old milk. I saw Jamil at the security, grabbed everything and headed downstairs.

Before I even opened Jamil's car door, I could hear Martha Wash's powerful soprano belting and telling me to look ahead and be unafraid. I smiled and in that moment knew that I was up against a bullshit situation.

There was no time to feel sorry for myself; I needed to deal with this and accept it. Better things will come, but for now, I had to roll with the punches. Jamil belted out the lyrics loudly as a way of greeting me; I hopped in the car and we left to deal with the chaos.

The gate was closed when we arrived at the office. I still had my keys but we were met by a security guard who had never stopped me before. He seemed polite but nervous.

'Are you Nadine?' he asked me while pulling a piece of folded paper from his pocket.

'Yes... I am,' I answered, clearly caught off guard.

He looked at me and bent down to look at Jamil in the car. He didn't seem like he had any intention of opening the gate and letting us in. He asked if he could just make a call. I was confused but agreed.

The security guard walked towards the gate and called someone. They spoke very briefly before he turned and walked back towards us.

I looked at Jamil and asked, 'What kinda kak is this?'

The security guard smiled politely and said, 'Uhm ... okay ... so Samantha says I must check off this list of the items you brought back.'

I was bewildered – she really blocked me from going inside and retrieving my belongings and didn't trust that there was a possibility that I would not steal from them. The security guard seemed to take no pleasure in it and kept saying, 'Askies, sisi.'

The black bag with my hopes and dreams sat on the pavement, my wound vacuum at my feet while we went over each item and checked it off the list. Everything down to a sim card inside the work-issued phone needed to be checked, T-shirts were checked by quantity, pencils and pens too. It was humiliating; I felt like a criminal who had been caught with stolen goods. She didn't even grant me a dignified handover; instead, I was bending down post operations to count used fabric masks.

Jamil sat there visibly outraged and even verbalising the ridiculousness of it all. Every day I try to imagine that we have progressed as a society, like we may have moved beyond blatant racist tactics and every day I am reminded to check my naivety at the door. I can't imagine that Samantha orchestrated the handover to be done in such an abrupt and humiliating way by chance. I don't believe she would do this to someone non-Black. After all she had an employee who worked for the organisation for years who she consistently called a different name because she didn't care to learn to pronounce the 'c' in isiXhosa. The entire show of getting a Black man to do her bidding while she surely watched on the camera was just a disgusting misuse of power. She needed to strip me of my dignity and personhood to teach me a lesson. I needed to be treated as a sketchy character in order to justify her outlandish behaviour.

A week later she sent me a message: 'Hi, Nadine. Susan has looked through the organisation's belongings and noticed that the phone's earphones were missing. Can you please return them immediately?' Of course, the white colleague didn't care to look for it before causing a scene over a pair of earphones for a cheap R800 Samsung. I was still on the mend and had put the gross display behind me, just grateful I didn't have to deal with them again and I didn't owe them shit. I looked at the message and read it repeatedly... 'The fucking audacity of this bitch,' I said in shock. Why on earth would I keep the earphones? They have no value; I never even used them – they were still wrapped up like the manufacturers package it, and in the phone's box, which I had returned as well. Clearly, they were just frantically looking for something I had failed to return. Logic would dictate that you would look in the box, right? I had had it with this woman and her penchant for soeking kak via text, calls and emails but never being brave enough to do so in person. I didn't have any grace left in my body for her bullshit; I couldn't even try.

I looked at the message again before writing a response: 'Oh, so because the white woman cries that something is gone, it is obviously the Black woman who stole it, right? Before she ran to you saying something was missing, did she bother to check the box it came in? Since I never used them, they very well are in that box. I am tired of being treated like a damn criminal. Before bothering me again with nonsense like this, make sure you've checked the box the earphones came in.'

I stared at the phone until the screen went black. I had truly reached the end of my threshold with this woman, the organisation, my health, the losses, finances, living in a city I only moved to because I was employed. It felt like the walls were closing in and I was struggling for air. My throat constricted as I held back tears, but the urge was too strong. I wailed and screamed until I couldn't anymore. I let it all out and finally felt like I could acknowledge the trauma I had just endured.

I just wanted to go home. I wanted to see familiar faces, I wanted to be cared for, I yearned to be able to rest without worrying about meals and other mundane responsibilities. All I wanted to do was see my family and friends and put this nightmare behind me. I felt like I hated Johannesburg because the so-called City of Gold had truly stolen everything from me. The city became a tangible thing I could blame for everything that had gone so horrifically wrong; I needed someone or something to blame.

I let my friends know I was leaving, and graciously they offered to help me pack up the comfortable little life I had created for myself. I felt their sorrow and pain, not only for me but also because I would leave. I quickly started to get the ball rolling: got movers, friends to help me pack, booked a flight, and took care of all admin beforehand. I anxiously watched my cosy life turn into an emptied wasteland. I had sold my couches and console and packed what I could manage into boxes and bags. My suitcases, rolled up carpet, black bags of my belongings and curtainless windows looked grim, but I knew I couldn't survive there. I knew it would kill me.

A last goodbye

BEING IN JOHANNESBURG MADE my skin crawl, I needed to get away. I wandered around my apartment the night before I was scheduled to hop on a flight and never look back – once a place filled with laughter, friendship and independence, now an empty, cold place filled with my ghost. I double checked everything to make sure nothing remained in the cupboards. I looked through the fridge once more, before eventually going to bed.

It was going to be a tough day. The movers were scheduled to arrive at 7 am sharp, and my flight only a few hours later. I must have passed out from exhaustion before jolting awake with panic. I needed to have my wound vacuum taken off before leaving for Cape Town. I sighed in relief when I opened my eyes and looked for it and realised it had already been removed a few days before and I was good to go.

The darkness throughout the room indicated it was still early morning. I grabbed my phone to check the time; it was 5:34 in the morning. I felt too nervous to go back to sleep. What if I overslept? I couldn't risk it. I stayed up in bed waiting for my alarm to go off so I could get up and get ready for what was to come. I felt weary, on edge and stressed beyond measure.

The past few months had truly zapped any source of comfort,

peace and happiness from me so curtly. The movers arrived a little bit after 7 am and they seemed clueless, like they didn't know where to start. They meandered around and shared quiet whispers with each other. I scowled in annoyance before barking, 'What is it? What's wrong now?'

One of the men in a blue overall looked over me, obviously surprised by my reaction. 'Uhm, ma'am, we don't have boxes or any packing material.'

Rage flew through me. What kind of moving company arrives with no packing materials? I called my mom in tears because I didn't know what to do. My mom listened attentively and asked me for the number of the person I had arranged the move with. I remembered that I still had a roll of black bags and cellotape. I quickly jumped up to get them.

'Here, I have black bags. Please pack whatever can be safely packed in these.'

They got to work packing things like pillows, clothes and curtains in the black bags. My phone rang and I quickly answered when I saw my mom's number. She had just gotten off the phone with the woman I made the booking with. The woman seemed as flabbergasted as we were to hear they had arrived with nary a box or tape.

In a calm tone, my mom let me know what was going on: 'Their manager says as soon as the shops open, they will need to go and buy materials.'

I sat down, feeling lightheaded. I would miss my flight if I needed to worry about the shops being open so they could pack my things. I also couldn't just leave them in the apartment and leave. I sat down on one of the chairs I was to ship and hyperventilated. I leant on the empty windowsill and teared up, watching the sun come out from behind the clouds.

Everything seemed to be going wrong again and I felt so defeated and fed up. I couldn't even think up a solution. I couldn't rebook my ticket for the following day because my things would be packed up. I looked down at the firm grip I had on my phone and decided to call Jamil. If anyone could talk me down and calmly handle the delays and mishaps it would be him, but the other side of me wondered if he would even be awake or available. I quickly dialled his number so there would be no chance for me to chicken out.

'Hello, salaaaams,' Jamil sang joyfully. I breathed out for the first time that morning.

I smiled feeling calmer. 'Hello, boo, look here, are you awake and able to come over and assist?'

Jamil didn't hesitate. 'Yes, of course, what do you need?' he asked.

Still teary I answered, 'I don't know… I just feel overwhelmed and the movers don't have packing supplies. I don't know what to do, and I am going to miss my flight,' I announced.

Jamil didn't ask any questions. I could hear him move around while on the phone, trying to get himself together to come to my aide.

'Okay, I will be there now now,' he said before we hung up.

I stayed in my position at the window, looking out for Jamil's arrival. I looked down and watched the movers carry my belongings to their truck. The fridge went first because they could wrap it in some grey itchy blanket. Others stayed in the apartment packing in an orchestra of whispers, the sound of cellotape being pulled and the shuffle of feet as they carried big items. I couldn't turn around; I couldn't face the mountain of belongings they still hadn't packed.

Jamil arrived fast, gliding past security and power walking in. My heart raced with nervousness. The door flung open and Jamil made his way to me. His demeanour was calm, cool and collected, all cozied up in an extra-long pink jersey coat over some tights and a long-sleeved top. I hugged him tight and found comfort in a familiar pleasant scent I associate with my best friend. He knew how I felt without my having to explain, but I hyper fixated on the fact that the movers came unprepared.

'How can they show up like this with nothing to pack my things in?' I scolded and motioned to all of my things now sitting on the floor that used to be my lounge.

'How can I leave like this? Everything will break, or spoil because they're not covered. I don't understand how they didn't bring any packing materials.' I harped on and on while Jamil sat silently, letting me vent. He nodded in agreement to make sure I felt heard before gently telling me how his childhood and the chaos he experienced at the hands of ill-prepared and ill-mannered adults taught him how to stay calm and solution-driven in times of unforeseen events.

'So, here is what I think. You should get done to go to the airport. I will stay here and make sure all your stuff gets packed.'

I sat and stared out of the window. I hated being a burden to anyone, and childhood trauma of neglect and being called a burden had truly fucked me up when it came to asking for or receiving help. I mulled it over, trying to think of different solutions, but I came up empty. I looked over and noticed Jamil had started to pack some things himself, making use of old bubble wrap and packing paper to protect things, putting valuables in pots and taping the lid shut, packing things into black bags with clothes and pillows to cushion it. I looked at him with such love and admiration because he meant it when he said he was calm and could help me. I marvelled at the resourcefulness of using a few old boxes of mine to reuse, making use of items that would not easily damage like my large rattan laundry basket, placing a piece of used plastic over the top and taping it shut.

I felt like my world was spinning off its axis. I watched the mountain of things in my used-to-be lounge evaporate but I still felt unsettled and like a live wire. The movers seemed to pick up on Jamil's methods and started doing the same, bringing large pieces of plastic from their truck to protect items. I worried about leaving Jamil alone in an apartment filled with what I can only assume were cishet men – I know how volatile they can be to queer folks. I just felt a responsibility to see it through somehow. I felt uneasy too because Jamil had been labouring for me for months now since my hospital stints. I felt like surely I have been asking for way too much from a friend. He owed me nothing and I couldn't take advantage of his kindness that had kept me alive, but no matter how I tried, I just wasn't in a state to be as independent as I usually am.

Jamil headed over to me at the window and said, 'I am going to stay here, and make sure everything gets packed well, and that the apartment is cleaned and the keys returned, don't stress about it. But you need to go to the airport now or you will miss your flight. Nanzugu.'

I couldn't help but burst into laughter at the utterance of the word 'nanzugu' but truly how fitting for the situation. Jamil's statement didn't feel like one for debate so I nodded and requested an Uber to the airport. My phone beeped loudly a few seconds later. 'Simon is 5 minutes away.' My body tensed up; 5 minutes felt so immediate.

Jamil grabbed my purple worn-out suitcase and carefully wheeled it to the door as I trotted behind him with my handbag and carry-on in tow. I felt a weird sense of melancholy, regret and heartbreak as we slowly made our way downstairs. I was glad I was going home but this final walk was painful. I loved living in such a beautiful and modern building and I particularly enjoyed the gold accents in their décor.

I kept telling myself not to look back as if I would turn into a pillar of salt. Simon was at the gate. I had to move if I wanted to make my flight. Jamil hugged me tightly, opened the door and helped me get my bags into the car. The adrenaline kept me from crying for the life I had built in Johannesburg. I looked at Jamil, so calm and collected.

'Thank you for everything,' I said.

He smiled and closed the car door, quickly turning on his heels, I suppose not to cry too. As Simon and I drove off I watched Jamil walk to the truck loaded with my belongings and grab a mop and bucket before they could pack it up. I wondered why for a moment; my thoughts felt muddled. 'Oh shit ... the apartment has to be cleaned top to bottom...'

I started to panic as we drove off because who would clean it? How would they know? I tried to think rationally and to rely on the people who had offered support. I exhaled. I assured myself that Jamil clearly knew it had to be done and we could make arrangements to have the place cleaned out one last time. The drive to the airport seemed especially long; the driver seemed to be taking detours through neighbourhoods I hadn't seen before. I checked the time on my phone, worried that I would miss my flight. I zoned out and looked out of the window. I wondered whether I was doing the right thing, whether this was it. I wasn't sure but I had to hold onto the fact that there was no turning back. This was it, the crescendo. My body ached in protest, my eyes felt sandy. I was kla, I just wanted to go home and get into my bed. I wanted to see my family and not worry about the small stuff.

The airport seemed unusually busy for a weekday morning but I shuffled through with my hefty suitcase and prayed I would make it on time. When I got to the counter, a young man told me with a joyful tone, 'You are just in time, we were just about to close the gates.'

I smiled awkwardly and tried to act natural even though I felt so overwhelmed – anything would set me over the edge and make me cry. I handed him my ID shakily; he looked at me with concern.

'Okay, there you go,' he said and smiled, handing me my ID and documents back. I smiled and thanked him meekly.

One more thing and then I am on a plane headed home. I just have to keep strong for one more task. I kept reminding myself it was just getting through security and then boarding the plane. I just kept walking and following the signs to get to my boarding gate. Everything else amalgamated and flew by me in my haste. When I sat down in my seat by the window, I finally found myself able to take a minute to myself and breathe. I looked out at the sun outside of my window. I smiled solemnly. I hoped that Cape Town would welcome me with a warmer sun, and a bluer sky. I tuned out the captain's announcements and other sounds and focused on holding my belly together – finally able to acknowledge my still raw abdomen.

I closed my eyes ... 'cerulean...' I thought to myself as the plane took off with a loud gust of air roaring in my ears. I kept my eyes closed, held my belly and hunched over ... 'cerulean...'

That was the colour I wanted to see when I got home – blue skies, blue ocean, blue hydrangeas. Cerulean is what home feels like.